Women in the Shadows

Ohio University Research in International Studies

This series of publications on Africa, Latin America, Southeast Asia, and Global and Comparative Studies is designed to present significant research, translation, and opinion to area specialists and to a wide community of persons interested in world affairs. The series is distributed worldwide. For more information, consult the Ohio University Press website, ohioswallow.com.

Books in the Ohio University Research in International Studies series are published by Ohio University Press in association with the Center for International Studies. The views expressed in individual volumes are those of the authors and should not be considered to represent the policies or beliefs of the Center for International Studies, Ohio University Press, or Ohio University.

Executive editor: Gillian Berchowitz
Southeast Asia Series consultants: Elizabeth F. Collins and William H. Frederick

Women in the Shadows

Gender, Puppets, and the Power of Tradition in Bali

Jennifer Goodlander

Ohio University Research in International Studies
Southeast Asia Series No. 129
Ohio University Press
Athens

To obtain permission to quote, reprint, or otherwise reproduce or distribute
material from Ohio University Press publications, please contact our rights and
permissions department at (740) 593-1154 or (740) 593-4536 (fax).

Printed in the United States of America

Previous versions of some of this research have appeared in publication
elsewhere.

The books in the Ohio University Research in International Studies Series
are printed on acid-free paper ⊚ ™

26 25 24 23 22 21 20 19 18 17 16   5 4 3 2 1

Library of Congress Cataloging-in-Publication Data
Names: Goodlander, Jennifer, 1975– author.
Title: Women in the shadows : gender, puppets, and the power of tradition in
Bali / Jennifer Goodlander.
Description: Athens : Ohio University Press, [2016] | Series: Ohio University
research in international studies. Southeast Asia series ; no. 129 |
Includes bibliographical references and index.
Identifiers: LCCN 2016026047| ISBN 9780896803039 (hc : alk. paper) | ISBN
9780896803046 (pb : alk. paper) | ISBN 9780896804944 (pdf)
Subjects: LCSH: Shadow shows—Indonesia—Bali Island. | Women
Puppeteers—Indonesia—Bali Island. | Wayang. | Sex role—Indonesia—Bali
Island. | Ethnology—Indonesia—Bali Island. | Bali Island
(Indonesia)—Civilization.
Classification: LCC PN1979.S5 G66 2016 | DDC 791.5309598/62—dc23
LC record available at https://lccn.loc.gov/2016026047

I dedicate this book in the memory of my mother.

Contents

Figures

Acknowledgments

Like any theater production, this research and the final written product resulted from the help and advice of many generous people. I especially wish to thank William F. Condee, who fostered my love of Balinese *wayang kulit*. He challenged me to use performance in my study and scholarship, which has provided insight and guidance through every step of this journey. I also thank Ed Menta for introducing me to Asian performance and challenging me to find connections between that and my interest in feminist theater and gender studies. This book is my response to that challenge.

I am grateful for wonderful colleagues at the University of Kentucky, Indiana University, and among the membership of the Association for Asian Performance (AAP). Andrew Kimbrough provided insightful comments on many versions of several chapters. Kathy Foley and the others at the AAP have given me invaluable advice and friendship. I am honored to be a part of such a wonderful community of scholars and artists who share my love of Asian performance. I heartily thank the reviewers of this manuscript for their thoughtful comments and the guidance of Gillian Berchowitz and Elizabeth Collins at Ohio University Press. Finally, I am so grateful for the supportive environment and wonderful colleagues at Indiana University in the Department of Theatre, Drama, and Contemporary Dance, the Mathers Museum of World Cultures, and the Center for Southeast Asia and ASEAN Studies.

I spent many months in Bali over a period of several years, developing the ideas and research that are contained in these pages. Such prolonged study would not be possible without generous financial support from many sources. The Graduate Student Senate of Ohio University awarded me a Research and Creative Activities grant, which partially funded my first trip to Bali. A Student Enhancement Award, also from Ohio University, gave me a second summer in Bali to study Balinese language and secure my research contacts. That trip was Gene Amaral's idea and I am grateful for his support. I then spent ten months in Bali, from December 2008 until October 2009, on a Fulbright Fellowship to Indonesia, which is an amazing program for cultural exchange and research. Elizabeth Clodfelter was instrumental in helping me with the application process. Finally, funding from the University of Kentucky and a Mellon Innovating International Research, Teaching, and Collaboration award from Indiana University allowed additional time in Indonesia.

I can't begin to express adequate thanks for my many friends, "family," and informants in Bali. The group Çudamani and Emiko Susilo introduced me to Balinese performing arts and culture. I Nyoman Sedana supported my application for the Fulbright, provided assistance along the way, and was the initial force behind my opportunity to perform at the Ubud Festival. I am extremely thankful for his wonderful advice and insight. Ni Made Murniati (called Kadek in this book) took me in as family, tirelessly led me around Bali, and answered my many questions. She and her family took care of me when I was sick or lonely and were the ones present to celebrate my successes. I am a better person for knowing her, her husband, and her children. At the arts university in Bali, Anak Agung Ayu Kusuma Arini served as my research counterpart and was extremely generous with her time and energy. I enjoyed watching her teach *gambuh* at the university, and I was honored to dance at a celebration at her house. I am indebted to the many other *dalang,* dancers, artists, and friends—too many to name—who influenced and helped me with my research. I must thank I Wayan Tunjung, my puppet teacher and dear friend. He and his family will always be close to my heart; words cannot express enough gratitude for all you have done for me. *Matur suksema.*

Finally, I thank my family for always believing in me. My father and mother spent countless hours driving me to rehearsals and performances; those hours are the foundation of my love for theater. My sister Kim has always been a great friend and confidant. She along with her husband, Dino, and children, Cooper and Natalie, fill my life with many riches. And finally, I want to acknowledge my partner, wife, and best friend, Tina. Thank you for sharing this adventure with me.

Note on Language and Terms

Research and writing about *wayang kulit* in Bali requires the use and study of several languages: Indonesian, Balinese, and Kawi. Spelling for these languages is not consistent among sources. In this book I use the *Tuttle Concise Indonesian Dictionary* (revised in 2006) and the *Tuttle Concise Balinese Dictionary* (2009) as my primary sources for those languages. Most of my research was conducted in Indonesian, and unless otherwise indicated all foreign terms are in Indonesian. For Kawi, I rely on the spellings and punctuation given to me by my sources in Bali. I am grateful to I Nyoman Sedana for his assistance with the Kawi and often providing translations.

When quoting another source I retain that source's spelling and capitalization, but otherwise I follow the practices advocated by the Association for Asian Performance, in which words for artistic genres, such as *wayang kulit,* should not be capitalized in the same way that their Western equivalents, such as *ballet,* would not be capitalized.

Wayang kulit has a specialized vocabulary that is difficult to replicate in English; therefore a few non-English terms such as *wayang kulit* or *dalang* will be used throughout this book. In Indonesian and Balinese, singular and plural noun forms are nearly always identical (e.g., *anak,* child, children). If a plural needs to be made clear, the word is spoken twice (e.g., *anak-anak,* children). Such plurals are awkward in English, so I often rely on context to indicate whether a word is singular or plural (e.g., "five women dalang"). When introducing a term for the first time, I include an explanation in the text. I have also included a glossary of non-English terms.

Chapter 1

GENDER, PUPPETS, AND TRADITION

If in the contest of colonial production, the subaltern has no history and cannot speak, the subaltern as female is even more deeply in shadow.
—Gayatri Chakravorty Spivak (1999, 274)

When I arrived at the house of my teacher, I Wayan Tunjung, a well-known *dalang,* or puppeteer, on the evening of January 17, 2009, it was already dark, even though it was just past seven. I was invited to accompany Pak Tunjung[1] to a shadow puppet, or *wayang kulit,* performance in Mas, a small village in southern Bali. Wayang kulit functions as a sacred ritual that mingles with religion and custom, as well as a social event with prescribed roles for all participants. Each performance is different, but I offer this description in order to give an example of the form and context of the tradition of wayang kulit.

I rode my *sepeda motor,* or motorbike, to Pak Tunjung's family compound. As always, when I went to a performance with Pak Tunjung, I wore *pakian adat,* the traditional clothing that, for a woman in Bali, means a sarong and a brightly colored *kebaya*—a type of blouse of lace or cotton with lace decoration. Around my waist I wore a sash of a contrasting color (fig. 1.1). Pakian adat—required for any temple ceremony, ritual, or important event in Bali—marks the performance as "special," or tied to traditional values and practices. Like all Balinese wearing this type of traditional

For anyone entering the Ubud Palace grounds, you must dress in

FULL ADAT (TRADITIONAL) CLOTHES

For Men:
Wastra - kain batik/sarong
Saput – worn over the wastra, with a sash to secure the wastra & saput
Baju – shirt (long or short-sleeved), **not a T-shirt or singlet**
Udeng – headdress, a square of white or batik material folded & tied around your head.

For Women:
Wastra – kain batik/sarong
Sabuk – A belt worn under the shirt to secure the wastra
Kebaya – Long-sleeved ladies shirt, **not a T-shirt or singlet**
Selendang – sash worn over the kebaya.

Figure 1.1. This sign explains the requirements for traditional clothes (*pakian adat*) for men and women in Bali. *Photo by author.*

clothing, I did not wear a helmet while on the motorbike, because the Balinese feel that a helmet is too modern and, as many Balinese explained to me, looks "wrong." My Balinese friends claimed that the law reflects this attitude by not requiring cyclists to wear a helmet with pakian adat; thus, at least discursively (if not actually), a separation between modernity and tradition is marked within both the social and the legal spheres.[2]

As I entered through the gate to the main courtyard of the compound, I was invited by Pak Tunjung to sit with him so we could talk about the performance he was going to give that evening. He contemplated which story to tell, explaining that a dalang knows many stories and must select the appropriate one for each situation. The performance that night was going to be at a family's compound for a tooth-filing ceremony, often called *matatah* in Balinese, or *potong gigi* in Indonesian, which is a coming-of-age ceremony in Bali (Eiseman 1989, 108–14). Wayang kulit provides entertainment while serving as a necessary ritual for many such ceremonies in Bali. The performance also operates as a marker of material wealth and power, because not every family can afford to hire a wayang kulit troupe for its personal rituals.

After Pak Tunjung and I chatted for about half an hour, the four musicians and two assistants, all men, arrived and began preparing for the performance. Even though the dalang is the spiritual and performative center of wayang kulit, he does not perform alone. The assistants carried the four musical instruments called *gender wayang,* the oil lamp, sound system, the box containing the puppets, and other equipment to the truck waiting outside the compound gate. Pak Tunjung checked his puppets earlier in the day to make sure he had the ones needed for the performance arranged within the puppet box. As the assistants were gathering the equipment, Pak Tunjung told them that he needed the crocodile puppet I had used earlier in the day for my lesson. One of the musicians took it from the puppet box I used for rehearsal and carefully placed the crocodile puppet in the box Pak Tunjung was going to use for the performance. Finally, Pak Tunjung went to bathe and get dressed. He had prayed and given offerings in his family temple earlier in the evening in order to recognize the gods and to ask for a successful performance. Pak Tunjung explained that the gods would guide his performance and provide protection from any troublesome spirits, or *ilmu penengen* (lit., black magic).[3] At around eight o'clock we piled into the van and headed on our way. I sat in the middle of the crowded front seat with the driver and Pak Tunjung, while the musicians, additional assistants, puppets, and equipment rode in the back. The location for this performance was only about ten minutes away, but sometimes Pak Tunjung would travel an hour or more to perform.

We climbed out after the truck pulled up in front of the family compound where the ceremony and performance were being held. I could hear the sound of a river running along the side of the narrow road. The men unpacked the vehicle while I followed Pak Tunjung through the gate that led into the compound. Once inside, a man came over to greet us and led us over to a *bale,* or covered platform, and we were asked to sit on a blue carpet. Soon, a man in a sarong and a mismatched batik shirt came over. He was a good friend of Pak Tunjung and they were happy to see each other. Later Pak Tunjung explained that since having his own family—a wife and a son—it was much harder to visit friends. When he was younger, Pak Tunjung would travel all night to give performances, often giving two or three in one evening, almost every night of the week. After his son was born, in 2006, he performed less often and preferred to stay closer to home. Often Pak Tunjung decided to accept a performance opportunity because it allowed him to see people he knew, exchange local gossip, and visit old acquaintances. Likewise, for many in attendance the performance provided an excuse to socialize, gossip, and eat together.

Social hierarchy is performed through language and actions[4] in Balinese society, and traveling with Pak Tunjung provided me with an opportunity to observe and participate in these exchanges. We hadn't been sitting long before several women approached and offered us coffee and *jaja,* little Balinese cakes made of rice and palm sugar. Pak Tunjung and I were provided with small individual trays with coffee and two cakes each, whereas the musicians and assistants shared one large common tray that had many coffees and cakes. The women smiled at me and said, "Silakan makan, silakan minum" (Please eat, please drink), as they set down the trays and hurried back to the kitchen area. Another tray was brought with cigarettes. One of the musicians gestured to the tray and made a joke of offering them to me with a smile, since it is not considered appropriate for a Balinese woman to smoke. They all laughed and grinned their approval when I refused the cigarettes. I waited to eat or drink until Pak Tunjung indicated that it was appropriate for me to do so. He ate and drank very little that night, and I remembered earlier he mentioned that his stomach was upset and he was worried about making it through the performance. Afterward he remarked to me that during the show he did not think about his stomach but only focused on telling the story and manipulating the puppets, attesting to how physically and mentally demanding the performance is for the dalang. Within the performance sphere, the dalang rises to the top of the social hierarchy: he is treated as an honored guest, he is valued for his wisdom and ability to perform, and he relaxes at the center of the compound, in a seat of honor while others prepare for the performance. My own presence at the event served as an interruption to the usual social hierarchy playing out through and around the performance. Unlike other women there, I did not help out in the kitchen or with serving. Like the other assistants, I was offered cigarettes, but my own refusal to take one pointed back to my womanliness. Like women dalang, I was disrupting the "usual" ways of doing things, but everyone made an effort to negotiate those boundaries in compliance with traditional social structures.

At approximately half past nine, we moved over to the compound's central bale, where the screen for the performance was assembled next to an elaborate altar with many colorful decorations and offerings. Behind the screen on a chain hung the oil lamp, and the puppet box and musical instruments were set in their places on the floor directly behind the screen. It was not a very large platform and I had to perch off to the side, next to the musicians. Several young boys and adults gathered around behind the screen to watch the dalang place the puppets, but in Bali most of the audience watches from the shadow side.[5] Figure 1.2 shows what it looks like behind the screen for a typical wayang kulit performance.

During the performance there are many things going on at once; rarely do people sit and observe with focused attention the way an audience would in the United States.[6] A group of young boys watched the beginning as the puppets were taken out of the box, but once the characters began talking, most of them wandered away. I could hear the sound of a video game being played nearby and it occurred to me that the beeping electronic music of the modern game made an odd contrast to the music and dialogue of the traditional puppet show. Scholars, visitors, and Balinese alike often wonder if wayang kulit will be able to compete with other

Figure 1.2. Backstage during a wayang kulit performance. *Photo by author.*

more technically advance modes of entertainment. These modern activities point to how traditional performance in Bali is changing and demonstrate how it also remains the same in many ways. The women were also missing from those watching the performance; they hardly had time to sit still, since they were working in the kitchen or adjusting the offerings. Old men were the most attentive audience members, and they sat in front of the screen on the ground and chewed betel nut as they watched. At one time or another, every person attending the event was drawn toward the screen like moths to a lightbulb. A group of younger men sat off to the side loudly talking and drinking tea during the performance; sometimes children would even run up and touch the screen or play with the puppets; women would stop in their tracks and take a moment to watch before rushing to the kitchen or family temple. It is never quiet during a wayang kulit performance.

Some parts of the performance attract the attention of a larger crowd of people. Sangut and Delem, two of the main clown puppet characters, or *penasar,* performed a scene full of jokes and slapstick that was one of the highlights of the performance. During the scene Delem described a recent experience he had going to the hospital and all the troubles he had there. The dalang used the comedy of the penasar to critique the troubled Indonesian medical system for being both expensive and inefficient. The audience's chatter erupted into laughter and cheers in response to the joking of the clowns. At one point everyone burst into applause at a clever remark made by Delem. The final scene of a performance is typically a fight scene with loud music and a great deal of action and can last up to an hour. Sometimes the puppets battle hand to hand and throw each other across the screen, and other times the puppets use arrows or other large weapons. As wayang kulit struggles to please a contemporary audience familiar with faster-paced movies and television, the comic and fighting scenes often dominate the performance over conventional themes of religion and moral philosophy.

After almost three hours of performance, the *kayonan,* or tree of life puppet, was returned to the center of the screen and the musicians played one last melody as Pak Tunjung and his assistants returned the puppets to the box. There was no applause, the audience just wandered away as soon as the penasar characters returned to make some final comments about the lessons that could be learned from the story told that night. Offerings were brought so that the dalang could bless the screen, the puppets, and the musical instruments by sprinkling holy water. Ritual significance permeates the performance and gives the dalang much of his power. At the end of the short ceremony, Pak Tunjung pulled out the center pin rooting the screen to the banana log to signify the end of the performance, and then he went off to the side to sit and talk with the sponsors of the performance. The musicians and the assistants folded the screen, gathered the sound equipment, and loaded everything into the van.

The work of the dalang is not over when the theatrical portion concludes. The sponsors thanked Pak Tunjung for the performance and gave him a small basket that contained several brightly colored flowers, rice, and money. Pak Tunjung counted the money, put it in his pocket, and tucked a yellow flower from the basket behind his ear. He often gave a small portion of the money back to the sponsor. This type of reciprocal exchange can be understood to reposition power from the sponsor to the dalang. Following a few more minutes of conversation, Pak Tunjung begged, "Permisi, mau pulang. Tamu saya capai" (Excuse us, we need to go home. The guest I brought is tired). Just as I benefited from traveling with Pak Tunjung, he often called attention to my presence to mark his performance as important on a global scale. We then stood, found our shoes, and returned to the van. Upon returning to Pak Tunjung's house, the assistants unloaded everything from the vehicle. I tried to help but they laughed at my efforts to carry the heavy equipment; it is not a job for a woman. As the final load was carried through the gate, I got on my motorbike to leave. Pak Tunjung reminded me, as he always did, to drive slowly and safely. Before going to bed, Pak Tunjung gave the puppets additional offerings and prayed to thank the gods for the successful performance.

Through my friendship with Pak Tunjung I was offered a privileged window into the world of Balinese culture; attending performances such as this one allowed me to witness firsthand the different components that constituted the tradition of wayang kulit, an opportunity complemented by my own practice of the art form. The many elements of the event—the people in the audience, the rituals that surround it, and the content of the story—all come together in a complicated tangle of tradition and modernity, gender, and performance.

The term *tradition* suggests an object or practice that has come, unchanged, from some mythical past into the present. Wayang kulit, or shadow puppetry, is often considered one of the oldest and most important traditions in Bali because it connects a mythic past to the present through public ritual performance. Flat, two-dimensional puppets, made out of carved leather, are manipulated against a screen by a single puppeteer to tell stories from the Mahabharata, Ramayana, or other Balinese myths and histories. These entertaining performances are generally given as an integral part of a ceremony or ritual. The dalang, or puppeteer, is the central figure in this performance genre and is revered in Balinese society as a teacher and spiritual leader.

Until recently, the dalang was always male, but now women in Bali are studying and performing as dalang. This innovation comes not without controversy because many people in Balinese society question women's ability to undertake the difficult physical and spiritual tasks of performing wayang kulit, as well as the appropriateness of a woman performing it. Women are rarely present in the audience or represented on the screen, thus making my interest in women dalang an anomaly among most considerations of wayang kulit. Women's roles in Balinese society have traditionally been in the sphere of the home, or in the shadows, and the opportunity presented within the shadows of wayang kulit offers an occasion to analyze how traditional performance creates and maintains systems of power in Balinese society.

Tradition is regulated by time and place; local, national, and international forces all contribute to the meaning and practice of traditions. Bali is a small island, located just east of Java and slightly south of the equator. Bali is part of Indonesia, which is made up of over seventeen thousand islands with over three hundred distinct ethnic groups and as many languages. Bali is less than one-third of 1 percent of Indonesia's land area of nearly 700,000 square miles (1.8 million km²), yet it is Indonesia's most popular destination. It has a tropical climate with a lush volcanic landscape in the south, dotted by terraced rice fields, and in parts of the west and east it is dry desert. Bali is one of Indonesia's most populous areas, with a population of over three million people, compared to the population of Indonesia, as of 2016, at almost 260 million. Tourism is the major source of economic revenue on the island, but historically people on Bali made their money through rice and trade (Pringle

2004, 1–5). Bali is the most visited and often the most recognizable part of Indonesia to foreigners.

Society in Bali is anything but homogeneous, as my use of the terms *Balinese society* or *the Balinese* may imply. Instead, when I use these terms, I am referring primarily to those who identify as Hindu, are ethnically Balinese, and live in the southern part of the island, where my research was conducted. I use the terms in order to both preserve clarity and put my work into conversation with other scholars writing about "the Balinese"; even so, I want to foreground this term as a conscious discursive construct rather than to erase the diversity of the people living on the island of Bali (Barth 1993, 9–15).

Scholars who write about women's performance in Bali often posit that women performers challenge Balinese tradition by taking nontraditional roles without accounting for how "tradition"[7] functions as a complex principle within Balinese arts and society. Catherine Diamond's work resonates with that of other women scholars (Bakan 1998; Susilo 2003; Palermo 2009; Downing 2010) by pointing to *gamelan wanita,* or women's gamelan, as one of several performance genres giving evidence of women's expanding gender roles in Bali. Middle-aged women especially find a "sense of accomplishment distinct from their other duties that are usually both never ending and taken for granted. Performance provides an opportunity to dress up, be involved, and sparkle artistically. It has raised their self-esteem, giving them an individual public identity other than being someone's wife or mother" (Diamond 2008, 235). Diamond, like the others, acknowledges limitations—in the end, art forms created and populated by mostly male performers perhaps can offer only partial opportunities for women to find their voice, and that until women create their own forms and characters they will experience only minimal representation (264). Cok Sawitri, a Balinese performance artist who borrows from tradition yet freely creates new and contemporary performance, is cited as an example of a woman managing to break gender norms through experimenting with new modes of performance (Vourloumis 2010;

Diamond 2008). Even so, the very nature of this kind of work places Sawitri at the margins, and her work has limited efficacy.

Inspired by these other publications on women and Balinese performance, I began my own study hoping to find that women performing as dalang would show a real departure from gender norms and indicate that the goal of equality was within reach. Instead, I found that women dalang have had little lasting impact on social hierarchy in Bali—and women dalang rarely, if ever, presently perform. I realized that in order to understand women dalang in Bali, and my own experience training as a dalang, I needed to better understand the notion of tradition in relation to gender and performance within Balinese society.

The idea of tradition in Bali is taken for granted as something from the distant and mythic past that functions as an important marker of identity and culture. Practices and things are designated as important because they are part of tradition. I approach the idea of tradition as both a taxonomic category and a cultural system to offer a richer, more complicated understanding of tradition in relation to gender in Balinese society as constituted within theatrical performance. In my analysis, the notion of tradition is used in relation to three different, yet overlapping, fields: the construction of Bali as a traditional society, the role of women in Bali as being governed by tradition, and the performing arts as both traditional and as a conduit for tradition. My focus is on Bali, but Balinese tradition exists within the nation of Indonesia, which also contributes to discourses and social meanings regarding gender and performance. I argue that the Balinese conception of tradition is not embedded in choreography or story, nor is it an object like a puppet, but rather tradition is a sign of power in the Balinese context through the meaning that society ascribes to those activities and objects. Therefore the concept of tradition in Bali must be understood as a system of power that is inextricably linked to gender hierarchy. The phenomenon of women dalang allows me to interrogate the complex dynamics of power in Balinese culture that are expressed through the performing arts. My analysis draws upon my own experience of the practical training and ritual initiation to become a dalang, coupled with interviews of early women dalang and leading Balinese artists and intellectuals. I unpack notions of tradition and gender as they relate to wayang kulit through examining practice, material objects, and ritual as they relate to systems of power.

Power as a concept in Indonesian society differs from how power is conceived in most Western cultures. Benedict Anderson, in his exploration of Javanese systems of power, provides a useful definition that applies equally well in the Balinese context. Anderson describes "power as something concrete, homogeneous, constant in total quantity, and without inherent moral implications as such" (1990, 23). This is in contrast to Western definitions, which see power as "an abstraction deduced from observed patterns of social interaction; it is believed to derive from heterogeneous sources; it is in no way self-limiting; and it is morally ambiguous" (22). In Bali, evidenced in wayang kulit, Anderson's notion of power permeates the aesthetics, performance, and social context of the performance—power is valued by its accumulation rather than its use. Shelly Errington (1990, 3–5) explains that this different system of power has made it difficult for scholars to understand gender relations in Southeast Asia because the systems of gender are not recognizable by Western standards. For example, in Bali both men and women wear sarong but they are not tied the same way. This difference is difficult to identify and understand without being able to "read" the social symbols. Wayang kulit provides a space to examine social systems of gender and power as they relate to tradition in Bali.

This book is divided into two parts in order to reflect the primary division of Balinese cosmology between the visible realm, or *sekala,* and the invisible realm, *niskala.* The first part—Sekala: The Visible Realm provides a detailed overview of the practices and objects of wayang kulit that emphasize the changing nature of the tradition. Chapter 2 examines the process of becoming a dalang by focusing on my own study of performing wayang kulit in order to establish the social nature of tradition as practiced within the performance. Folklorist Barry McDonald proposes that tradition is "the human potential that involves personal relationship, shared practices, and a commitment to the continuity of both the practices and the particular emotional/spiritual relationship that nourishes them" (1997, 60). Building on this definition and drawing on the work of Pierre Bourdieu, I analyze my own experience of studying this art for more than a year in Bali in order to frame wayang kulit as a practice that reflects the dynamic social and cultural dimensions of the performance and of the concept "tradition."

Chapter 3 builds on this work and describes and analyzes the objects that are required for a wayang kulit performance, such as the puppets, the puppet box, and musical instruments, together with the less tangible objects (i.e., skills), important for a performance such as the voice, the music, and the stories told. Throughout the chapter, I emphasize how these objects function as material culture that relates to economic and social capital. For example, I examine the puppet box as one of the most important markers of a dalang, discuss my own process acquiring a box, the criteria for determining its quality, and how frequent use is an important part of its value as a traditional object.

The second part of the book—Niskala: The Invisible Realm— examines the many invisible realms of power expressed through and beyond the performance of wayang kulit. Chapter 4 begins with my invitation to perform wayang kulit at the Ubud Festival in August 2009. Thus my role changes from being a student and researcher to *becoming* a dalang and details the transformative spiritual process I underwent. I describe the rituals and ceremonies necessary to give a performance and also problematize the relationship of identity and spirituality in Bali in regard to tradition and power as I, a foreigner and a woman, begin to occupy this unique position in Balinese society.

Chapter 5 examines how the recent phenomenon of women dalang manipulates invisible realms of ritual and social power through the tradition of wayang kulit. I examine relationships between government institutions and ritual performance in order to contextualize the practice of women dalang within the greater arena of gender relations and traditional performance, especially as these relate to national agendas of modernization. I look closely at the initial opportunity for women to study wayang kulit made by I Nyoman Sumandhi, the then head of the Balinese performing-arts high school. The chapter contains interviews with Pak Sumandhi and five of the most prominent women dalang to perform in Bali.

The final chapter examines a new performance I learned that tells the story of Gugur Niwatakwaca. This story features several female characters and offers an opportunity to put gender in conversation with the invisible and visible realms of wayang kulit to better understand how women dalang point to gender in Balinese society into the future.

Part One

SEKALA:
THE VISIBLE REALM

Chapter 2

PRACTICES OF
TRADITION

*Art cannot be taught. To possess an art means to
possess talent. That is something one has or has not.
You can develop it by hard work, but to create a
talent is impossible.*
— Richard Boleslavsky 2005, 1

The Tradition of Wayang Kulit

The practice and significance of Balinese performance constantly changes over time. I Made Bandem and Fredrik Eugene deBoer (1995) describe how variance and innovation flourished in the twentieth century with the professionalization of performers, influences from foreign artists and audiences, expanding tourism, the formation of the nation, and the natural creativity of Balinese artists. Some forms become popular and remain as new "traditions," while others may exist for only a brief moment. In Bali, art forms exist and move along a dynamic scale between religious and secular, or *kaja* and *kelod* (indicating the mountain and the sea respectively). Constant adjustments within arts reflect Balinese cosmology, which favors balance and harmony, or *rwa bhineda*. The relationship is circular—"while the performing arts themselves are also subject to social change, acts of performance are simultaneously employed to further the understanding of what constitutes harmony in the modern world as well as restore it" (Diamond 2012, 92). Tradition changes to mirror a continuously evolving society.

Since the start of the twenty-first century, the idea of tradition has undergone several notable changes in Bali. Tradition as vital to Balinese societal well-being came sharply into focus after the bombings in a Kuta nightclub on October 12, 2002. Many writing for the press and within the government felt that the Balinese had suffered this calamity because they had wandered too far from traditional values, religion, and culture and that in order to both heal and move forward the Balinese must look to the past. This return to the past has been dubbed *ajeg*,[1] a word that is difficult to translate directly, but now the emphasis on balanced harmony stresses stasis rather than fluid change. Ajeg Bali has been invoked in order to justify architectural styles, religious imperatives, gender relations, political movements, and recently the term is used in discriminatory actions against the large number of immigrants from other parts of Indonesia who are looking to share in Bali's thriving economy. Ajeg is not so much a longing to return to the past but rather a desire for stability in an era of rapid change. Tradition, then, becomes a litmus test for and marker of that stability. Of course, not all Balinese subscribe to the ajeg Bali doctrine, and I did not directly encounter the term in relation to wayang kulit during the course of my research. However, it is necessary to mention it here as part of a larger conversation within Balinese society as it struggles to maintain unique identity and values against many different forces including tourism, Indonesian nationalism, globalization, and modernization.

Traditional performance provides the Balinese a means for situating themselves in relationship to the world. Performance is often synonymous with culture in Bali. Angela Hobart offers the typical view of wayang kulit as tradition:

> It is the most esteemed and conservative theatre form and hence its dramatic and aesthetic principles link it to other dance-dramas, statues, reliefs, and traditional painting. Of

these the shadow play is regarded as the original form. Through these various manifestations the villager is able to probe and analyze his assumptions of self, in a world which is increasingly affected by modern trends, while retaining his human dignity. (1987, 14–15)

In practice, wayang kulit as tradition means that each performance follows certain conventions and structures.[2] At night, Balinese wayang kulit is performed against a screen made of white cloth that measures about six feet across and is outlined in a red or black border.[3] The dalang, or puppeteer, brings his own screen to the performance area, where the sponsoring family or village has either constructed a booth or erected a stage for the performance (fig. 2.1), and a frame is built out of bamboo for the dalang to affix his screen and hang his lamp. The dalang sticks his puppets into or

Figure 2.1. The assistant hangs the screen in preparation for a wayang kulit performance. *Photo by author.*

leans them against the banana logs along the bottom and sides of the stage. Although electricity is sometimes used, an oil lamp that hangs right in front of the dalang's face is still the preferred method of illumination. A microphone now is commonly affixed to the lamp to amplify the dalang's voice. Four gender wayang, small metallophones, typically accompany the performance, although some genres of wayang will use a larger gamelan ensemble. Musicians and assistants sit behind and to the side of the dalang while most of the audience watches the shadows projected onto the other side of the screen. Each of these elements is symbolic: the screen is the world; the puppets are all the physical and spiritual things that exist in that world; the banana log is the earth; the lamp is the sun—it allows there to be day and night; the music represents harmony and the interrelationships of all things in the universe; and the dalang, invisible behind the screen, resembles a god presiding over everything (Hobart 1987, 128–29).

Wayang kulit is often described by other scholars, as well as many of the Balinese I met, as a microcosm of Balinese society, culture, and ideals, because a wayang kulit performance instructs its audience on matters of morality, politics, and philosophy. Wayang kulit also functions as a form of offering to the gods. Balinese Hinduism divides the world into three parts: the lower realm of "bad" spirits, or demons; the middle realm that we live in; and the upper realm of the "good" spirits, or gods (Lansing 1983, 52). Balinese cosmology does not privilege gods over demons in the same way Christianity does, because there is no struggle for one side to eventually win out over the other. Instead there is a recognition of the importance of both kinds of power; much of Balinese religious activity, including wayang kulit, is centered on bringing these opposing forces into balance. Anthropologist Stephen Lansing explains how wayang negotiates religious forces within Balinese society:

> To create order in the world is the privilege of the gods, but the gods themselves are animated shadows in the wayang, whom the puppeteers call to their places as the puppeteers

assume the power of creation. . . . puppeteers are regarded by the Balinese as a kind of priest. However, they are priests whose aim is not to mystify with illusion, but rather to clarify the role of illusion in our perception of reality. As Wija [a well-known dalang] explained: "Wayang means shadow, reflection. Wayang is used to reflect the gods to the people, and the people to themselves." Wayang reveals the power of language and imagination to go beyond "illumination." To construct an order in the world which exists both in the mind and, potentially, in the outer world as well. (1983, 82–83)

It is important to remember throughout my account of wayang that it maintains this complex nature: the puppeteer is understood to be speaking for the gods and to the gods; he also functions as a kind of god himself because he has called the world of shadows into being.

Becoming a Dalang

The dalang is the ultimate performer because he[4] is the one that manipulates the tradition within a wayang kulit performance and ensures that all the elements of the performance work together. He is the playwright, actor, director, orchestra conductor, musician, singer, producer, and priest all combined into one artist. He needs to be an expert in Balinese philosophy, religion, politics, and myth, as well as a talented storyteller and comedian. The dalang's skill as a performer, together with his knowledge and perceived wisdom, make him a respected member of Balinese society. It takes a lifetime to master the art of wayang kulit, and a respected dalang is always seeking to improve his knowledge or skill.

In the past, only the son or grandson of a dalang could study wayang kulit. The knowledge about the performance passes down from one generation to the next in many formal and informal ways. For example, Nandhu, my teacher's son, often sat nearby or on his father's lap during my lessons. He was just a toddler but had paper puppets and a few small leather ones to play with. In general, children or others are not allowed to touch the "real," or sacred, wayang; they can only be handled by a dalang or a student, usually an adult, of a dalang. Nandhu learned about the performance through watching his father, through play, and by telling stories with his father. Sometimes an eager youngster might be taken in by a dalang who is not his father, and the student becomes like a son to his teacher and is called *anak murid,* or child-student.

A major evolution in the process of becoming a dalang has been through the opportunity to study wayang kulit at the Sekolah Menengah Karawitan Indonesia (SMKI), the high school for the performing arts, and at the Institut Seni Indonesia (ISI), the arts university.[5] This method of training introduces older would-be dalang to different styles and teaches a couple of the basic stories. A professor in the program, I Nyoman Sedana (1993, 24) notes that for a dalang to really be successful, he must seek additional training outside formal education in high school or university.

My own experience and relationship with my teacher can be understood as a combination of formal education in the university and working with a dalang as a kind of anak murid. My study of wayang kulit began at the University of Hawai'i and continued at Ohio University, but like the aspiring dalang in Bali, this was not enough. I needed what folklorist Barry McDonald (1997, 64) describes as a "personal relationship" where "emotion, commitment, and deep communication are all crucial entities" in order to understand the tradition of wayang kulit as social action and artistic practice.

I found my "personal relationship" through a chance meeting. My partner, Tina,[6] and I had been in Bali only a week, and we arrived in Ubud just in time for a large royal cremation (the largest ever, many papers proclaimed). The sarcophagi were so big that the villagers had not been able to burn them right away, so we returned to the graveyard a couple of days later to see the fires before they completely died out. Intrigued to know more about the cremation, we began chatting with a local Balinese man named Jaga, who was sitting there watching the activity around him. Jaga told us that they had started the fires late at night on the day of the procession and that the cremation towers were still smoldering. He asked what we were doing in Bali, and I explained that I came here to study culture and the arts, *kesenian dan budayaan.* When Tina mentioned that I hoped to find someone with whom to study wayang kulit, Jaga said he knew a dalang who would be an excellent teacher. Jaga offered to introduce us to him; I decided it was worth investigating and we agreed to meet.

The next morning Jaga met us at our hotel and drove us to Pengosekan, an area in the southern part of Ubud that is known for its strong community of artists. Jaga pulled the car to the side of the road and we walked through the narrow gate that is the typical entrance into a Balinese home. Traditional homes in Bali consist of several small buildings situated around a garden. We passed a statue of Ganesha, the god of wisdom and learning, to be welcomed by a spry-looking man sitting within the central *bale,* or pavilion. The man, I Wayan Tunjung—or Pak Tunjung, as I would come to call him—welcomed us and asked us to join him sitting on the mat. We drank sweet tea and talked about my desire to study wayang kulit. Pak Tunjung seemed pleased to meet me and eager to take me on as a student; he promised that he would teach me "systematically" and said that I could also learn to carve puppets. We agreed to begin classes the following week and we would meet on Monday, Wednesday, and Friday mornings. When I asked about payment he said that he worked for the love of his art and culture—he did not have a set price. We would figure it out.

I was not the first and certainly will not be the last foreigner to study arts in Bali through a close personal relationship with one or more teachers. Foreigners have a long history of working with Balinese artists—allowing for what Stephen Snow terms "deep learning," that is, "learning that takes place on all levels: in the mind, heart, and body" (1986, 204). Snow examines the work of Islene Pinder, who studied dance; John Emigh, who studied *topeng;* and Julie Taymor, who collaborated with several Balinese performers, as examples of three artists who spent extended time in Bali learning and performing to bring those influences into their artistic practice. The benefits, echoing Dwight Conquergood's (1985, 9–11) notion of "dialogical performance," allow the artist to successfully negotiate cultural and aesthetic differences to bring a performance genre from one context to another. The idea of "deep learning" could also be applied to Ron Jenkins, Colin McPhee, Carmencita Palermo, Margaret Coldiron, and others who have dedicated a portion of their life and work immersed in Balinese performance. Larry Reed studied Balinese wayang kulit, first with I Nyoman Sumandhi in California and then in Bali with Sumandhi's father, Pak Rajeg, in Tunjuk. Reed built on that experience to create innovative productions mixing shadow puppets and live actors with his theater company, ShadowLight. Reed's work attempts not only to transmit Balinese theater forms to an international audience but also to "make it his own" (Diamond 2001, 260). Several scholars who study, perform, and write about other types of puppetry in Indonesia deserve mention. Matthew Isaac Cohen performs Javanese wayang kulit and Kathy Foley performs Sundanese *wayang golek;* both are masters of the form who draw from their performance experience to enhance their scholarship. The study of wayang "has been possible for foreigners, even actively encouraged, since the 1960's" (Cohen 2014, 190). Many Balinese also have come to the United States and other countries abroad to work, teach, and learn. Pak Tunjung's own teacher, I Wayan Wija, has toured the world and embarked on several collaborations with international artists.[7] My own experience must be understood as part of a larger international exchange and flux of ideas regarding Balinese performance and wayang around the world.[8]

For the rest of the summer and then the following year, those Mondays, Wednesdays, and Fridays became the foundation of my slow initiation into wayang kulit. I have returned to Bali many times to continue learning and to add to my repertoire of stories and knowledge. Often during our lessons or at performances, Pak Tunjung would implore me to remember to honor the tradition of wayang kulit—to perform it "the Balinese" way. He would come up with ideas for my performances; for example, he proposed that instead of the traditional oil lamp, I should get a hat and put different colored lights on it, because I could then light my screen with blue, red, white, or yellow light depending on the mood of the scene. I also went with Pak Tunjung to watch him perform at a variety of ceremonies and events, where many of the Balinese I met would comment that they liked his performances because he was a very "traditional" performer. Sometimes I would watch Pak Tunjung perform *wayang tantri,* a new form of wayang made famous by one of Pak Tunjung's teachers, the aforementioned Pak Wija from Sukuwati, which features dynamic animal puppets that were designed specifically for this performance.[9] Pak Tunjung often told me stories from the Mahabharata[10] and reminded me that it was important for a dalang to know these tales and be able to tell them well. He also described new performances he was creating using other stories or myths from the history of Bali. These discussions and examples demonstrated how "tradition" functions as an affect, or a "process of continual creation of meaning" (Guattari 1996, 159), rather than a stable category. The tradition of wayang changes over time and varies within the present.

As I continued learning wayang kulit, I kept wondering about what it meant to study a "traditional" performance genre. How is tradition constituted through the actions of different individuals? What did it mean for me, an American and a woman, to study this tradition? How might I fit within and outside Balinese social structures? Over time I became a dalang and Pak Tunjung became a kind of older brother to me; through examining this process I better understand how wayang kulit is connected to society and my own place within the tradition.

Tradition, Practice, and Society

I understand wayang as a practice of training and performance that connects to larger Balinese social spheres. The word *practice* suggests several different meanings, and I purposefully use the term in this multidimensional way. One meaning refers to the practice that it takes to learn a skill, such as learning to play tennis or speak a foreign language. In theater, the definition of "rehearsal" is to practice in order to learn a play. Sociologists have extended the meaning of *practice* to include the activities we do in everyday life, or our "ways of operating," which "constitute the innumerable practices by means of which users reappropriate the space organized by technics of sociocultural production" (Certeau 1984, xiv). Practice, therefore, implies repetition connected to and affected by social hegemonies that are enacted through the body. Diana Taylor names this connection between learned bodily knowledge and society the "repertoire," which unlike written or documented knowledge, "enacts embodied memory: performance gestures, orality, movement, dance, singing—in short, all those acts usually thought of as ephemeral, nonreproducible knowledge." The key is in the doing, because "the repertoire requires presence: people participate in the production and reproduction of knowledge by 'being there,' being part of the transmission" (2003, 20). McDonald focuses the study of tradition on transmission by proposing that "tradition" is "the human potential that involves personal relationship, shared practices, and a commitment to the continuity of both the practices and the particular emotional/spiritual relationship that nourishes them" (1997, 60). Practice therefore provides a means for thinking through how performance traditions are connected to social spheres. Tradition, such as wayang kulit, operates within the body and is passed along from one body to another—reverberating within society.

I want to focus on the moment of transmission as key for unpacking how tradition functions as practice and connects to the greater structures of power within a society. The theories of Pierre Bourdieu, as he is concerned with "the mode of generation of practices," highlights the relationship between what people do and systems of hierarchy within their society. Bourdieu describes society's overlying system as habitus:

The structures constitutive of a particular type of environment (e.g. the material conditions of existence characteristic
of a class condition) produce *habitus,* systems of durable,
transposable *dispositions,* structured structures predisposed
to function as structuring structures, that is, as principles of
the generation and structuring of practices and representations which can be objectively "regulated" and "regular"
without in any way being the product of obedience to rules,
objectively adapted to their goals without presupposing a
conscious aiming at ends or an express mastery of the opera-
tions necessary to attain them and, being all this, collectively
orchestrated without being the product of the orchestrating
action of a conductor. (1977, 72)

Habitus, for Bourdieu, is created through primarily unconscious
action, or action that because of the "natural" way it is experienced
seems to be unconscious. I propose that if habitus is executed
through repeated behaviors, therefore "tradition" is a way of iden-
tifying one of these kinds of behaviors. Because tradition singles
out behaviors or items as having particular meaning in society,
tradition is therefore related to the structures of society in an efficacious way. The source of the tradition need not be traceable, and the
history of wayang kulit is likewise difficult to recount, so therefore
wayang kulit must be studied in the moment of generation as it is
passed from teacher to student. So, just as the structures of habitus
"are determined by the past conditions which have proceeded the
principle of their production" (ibid.), the tradition of wayang kulit
is also produced and determined in relationship to the established
aesthetics and content of the performance.

Learning a theatrical system physically and mentally, or spiritually, changes the student. Richard Schechner describes how the
study of *noh, kathakali,* or ballet involves "learning new ways of
speaking, gesturing, moving. Maybe even new ways of thinking
and feeling"; the form changes the body through diligent training
and practice, thus "deep, permanent psychophysical changes are

wrought." The performer becomes a *shite,* the character of Rama, or a dancer and this process changes the performers way of being and relating to the world around him or her—"they are marked people" (1993, 257). Schechner notes that the student brings a blank slate, a tabula rasa, to the training because many of these initiates start learning their craft at a very young age. I, however, began studying wayang kulit as an adult and my exposure to the art form was limited before I arrived in Bali.[11] Even so, the bodily experience of learning the form changed me. I was left to wonder, as an outsider, how do I participate in and contribute to Balinese arts and "tradition"? What implications does my participation have for forming a definition of "tradition" in Bali?

Kathy Foley, writing from her own experience learning wayang golek, or rod puppetry, in West Java provides an explanation for the kind of "Balinese" character I could occupy. She writes that learning to perform with the puppets and masks allows performers to "multiply their bodies" through the performance, and that "through the one body we inhabit in this life we can, with the help of these puppets or masks and the ideas they encode, embody the whole cosmos" (1990, 61). The body changes because learning to use puppets begins "by moving away from oneself," unlike many systems of actor training that begin from the actor's own personality and life history (65). One of the women dalang I interviewed explained the different skills necessary to perform wayang kulit: "If you are going to perform wayang it is important to practice it all. You need to practice the voice, dancing the puppets, and the foot also. You must become one [*menyatu*] with the puppets. It is very important. It is important to be able sing and do the voices" (Trijata 2009).Whether in Java or Bali, the performer in puppet theater must learn to physicalize, vocalize, and think a variety of characters that are connected to society through the myths those characters embody and the culture that informs them. Performance provides insight into tradition, as Henry Glassie states: "the performer is positioned at a complete nexus of responsibility" and as such must account for his teachers, the audience, and himself

(1995, 402). I inserted myself into the structures of Balinese society by working within the system of the performance tradition. Foley writes, "I feel that my body is still open to the meanings of the practice in itself. Indeed, practice is the only way to get beyond the simple introductions that are found in books and the fragmented, albeit tantalizing information about meanings that come from performers" (1990, 77).[12]

That I had changed as a result of my experience was noticed by others as well; as this story illustrates: "Om swastiastu!" I called out to my friend Eka as he walked down the path to where I was living in Bali. We met at Ohio University when he was a student there and I was taking my graduate coursework. Now, after living for a few years in Washington, DC, Eka was back in Bali, and after seven months of fieldwork, I was happy to see a familiar face. "Om swastiastu," he responded with surprise in his voice. "Om swastiastu" is a Balinese rather than Indonesian greeting, typically not known by foreigners. "You speak Balinese?" Eka asked me. "Abidik sajaan," I answered in Balinese, meaning "only a little." Eka laughed as he came up the stairs to my balcony. We sat at a little table and sipped hot tea while Eka admired the view of the garden and rice fields that I had from my room. We talked about my research in Bali and I told him I had studied dance and performed at a couple of temple ceremonies. He was especially curious about my experience with wayang. He peppered me with questions: "Do you perform in Kawi? What story are you doing? Are you using an oil lamp? What kind of music? Do you have your own puppets? How often do you go to the temple? You mean you are learning to make the puppets, too?" Eka was truly surprised with all I had been doing. Finally, before he left, he exclaimed with a smile, "My goodness! You are more Balinese than me!"

On the one hand, I knew Eka's comment was purely out of friendly admiration for all I had been learning and doing over the past year, as there are a lot of foreigners in Bali but very few of them learn Balinese language or spend time doing "Balinese" things. Eka's words also reflected an awareness that many more

Balinese, like himself, are spending less time doing traditional performance and art; the artists I spent my time with do not represent "typical" Balinese. Many people in Bali work in hotels, shops, or for the government and do not make their living as dancers, puppeteers, or musicians. Young people prefer television to topeng and like pop music better than gamelan. Eka's exclamation, which I received occasionally in some form or another from other Balinese people, reflects a perception, however, that language, culture, and the arts, especially wayang kulit, play a role in the formation of a "Balinese" identity.

Teachers in Bali transmit knowledge and skill of performance to their students through the body. Students stand alongside or behind their teachers to copy movements—teachers will often physically adjust or move their students into the correct pose. The process is not always easy. Emigh describes the difficult nature of his own training in topeng: "daily [my teacher, I Nyoman Kakul] wrench[ed] my resistant body into something approximating the proper shapes for Balinese dance" (1979, 12). I often observed dance teachers with their Balinese students use their hands to adjust a dancer's hip, head, hand, or leg. If I made a mistake in executing a motion with the puppet, my teacher, Pak Tunjung, would take my hand so he could guide my body and make my movements more precise. Likewise, Pak Tunjung would sometimes sit with his son, Nandhu, on his lap and guide his hand holding the puppet across the screen (fig. 2.2). This is a typical method of teaching in Bali, regardless of age and gender of the students. Jonathan McIntosh describes how a Balinese dancer first learns visually by copying, but then the movements are refined through direct transfer, "the teacher will frequently take hold of a student by wrapping his or her arms around those of the student. . . . Through this process the teacher's style of dancing and interpretation is kinaesthetically transferred to the student" (2006, 7). One body has power over the other to transfer knowledge of tradition.

Pak Tunjung's willingness to teach me, body to body, greatly enhanced my ability to learn and to understand the nuanced

Figure 2.2. Pak Tunjung teaches his son, Nandhu, how to perform wayang kulit—the tradition is passed through the body. *Photo by author.*

movement of the puppets. The first time he took my hand, however, he hesitated, and asked, "I will show you, OK?" Age, gender, and ethnicity might have been a factor in his initial hesitation,[13] but the question could also be understood as an invitation to fully inhabit the bodily knowledge of the tradition. The student grants the teacher power over his or her body.

Because I learned wayang kulit in my body, the body offers an ideal site for studying the relationship between the past and present as expressed and experienced through tradition. Maurice Merleau-Ponty observes, "The present still holds on to the immediate past without positioning it as an object, and since the immediate past similarly holds its immediate predecessor, past time is wholly collected up and grasped in the present" (1962, 80). People constantly put themselves in relation to objects and time, just as these things are positioned relative to them—the body remains the primary point of reference. Tradition, like habitus, relates to the past, but also like habitus this does not mean tradition reproduces exactly from generation to generation. People improvise interactions within their social situations according to a set of rules and expectations,[14] much like a dalang improvises each individual performance according to set rules and expectations. Bourdieu (1977, 73, 76–77) argues that practice within the habitus is neither mechanic or predetermined, nor is it completely a matter of free will, rather that actions or strategies of any individual or group are always conceived and executed within the structures that surround them, and that actions are thus limited by the available possibilities. Bourdieu's explanation of this situation could certainly apply to how tradition functions as well:

> This is why generation conflicts oppose not age-classes separated by natural properties, but habitus which have been produced by different *modes of generation,* that is, by conditions of existence which, in imposing different definitions of the impossible, the possible, and the probable, cause one group to experience as natural or reasonable practices or aspirations which another group finds unthinkable or scandalous, and vice versa. (78)

My own study of wayang kulit provides an excellent point of departure for pinpointing the structures of the performance and its relationship for society because of the level of learning that I needed to undertake as a foreign woman. An examination of the practice of wayang kulit and later of women dalang allows me to identify the conditions and properties that apply to tradition and to Balinese society on a larger scale. Practice gives me a vocabulary for explaining how tradition has expanded or changed to allow this "unthinkable practice," of women dalang, to emerge as well as supposing how women dalang might fit into the larger structures of Balinese society and whether this expansion has caused any notable change in the gender hierarchy.

Structures

The structure of a typical wayang kulit performance can often be broken into three parts, or three acts.[15] The opening scenes include an invocation to the gods, inviting them to watch and participate in the performance. Next, the main characters enter to introduce the story, which the clowns, or penasar, Twalen and Merdah will translate and comment upon. There might be an additional traveling scene (*angkat-angkatan*) or love scene (*rebong*) before the next major act division, which will introduce the antagonist characters. The penasar Delem and his thin brother, Sangut, dominate this scene with their often raucous jokes and antics. The third act provides an arena for the two sides to meet and do battle; it is the climax of the performance. The performance ends with the penasar expressing their gratitude for the patience of the audience and offering the moral or lesson of the story. The dalang then closes the performance with a final ritual dedication, and sometimes he conducts the ceremony to make holy water.[16]

Arjuna Tapa (Arjuna's meditation) is a popular story for young dalang to use to learn the practice of wayang kulit, and it is the first story that I learned to perform. In this story Arjuna sets out for the top of the mountain Indra Kila Giri because he is troubled by the war between his brothers, the Pandawas, and their cousins, the Korawas.[17] Arjuna worries many people will die because of this war between his family members. At the top of the mountain Arjuna seeks wisdom through offerings to the gods and meditation, so that he might imagine a solution to this problem. Arjuna's journey up the mountain is not easy; he faces many dangers because he is traveling where few others have gone before. Additionally, his desire for wisdom has made the ogre king, Niwatakwaca, angry. Arjuna does not find peace, and must battle for his life on the mountain, yet eventually the god Indra helps Arjuna by giving him a powerful weapon to destroy his enemies. At the end of the story, Arjuna is whisked away to the heavens, where he will find wisdom and more adventures.

I will use the three-part structure of wayang kulit as a description of my learning experience and as an analytic tool. The first section will focus on the basic aesthetics that are expressed and maintained in a wayang kulit performance. The second section will explore the character of the clowns and how comedy functions as a vehicle for "freedom" and social commentary, even within the set aesthetics and structure. Finally, I will describe the reception of my work, which sometimes caused conflict, in order to connect the practice of learning wayang kulit to practices within Balinese society and ritual. A wayang kulit performance contains action, narration, and commentary; likewise each section contains all these elements.

Part One—Aesthetics

A wayang kulit performance always begins with the *kayonan,* a large leaf-shaped puppet with intricate carving, in the middle of the screen (fig. 2.3). This puppet, often called "the tree of life" in English, is a symbol of "creative and imaginative forces" (Zurbuchen 1987, 32); it marks the beginning and ending of the performance, it indicates shifts between the three main parts, and it can be used as a transformative prop such as wind, fire, or a chariot. Mary Sabina Zurbuchen explains that the imagery and use of the kayonan in performance "links the dalang to other Balinese ritual specialists who also have access to the 'unmanifest' world" (134). The kayonan presents the narration of the play, blurring the distinction between the dalang's voice and mythic voices of the ancestors represented within the ornate puppet.

At my first lesson, even without a screen, Pak Tunjung taught me how to hold the kayonan between my thumb and fingers so that I could control the movement with my entire hand. Next I learned the first of two kayonan "dances" that begin the performance. I began by holding the kayonan close to my face, and in those moments my breath slowed. As I listened to the music being played

Figure 2.3. The kayonan puppet begins the performance at the center of the screen. *Photo by Tina (Cox) Goodlander.*

by the gender wayang (Gending Pamungkah), my awareness of my surroundings dissipated—I created a connection with the puppet and was thus prepared to perform. Using the *cepala,* a small wooden hammer held in the hand or toes, which I clutched in my left hand, I knocked slowly on the puppet box and then knocked faster and faster. Pak Tunjung taught me that the knocking begins in time with the music and then as it gathers energy it surpasses the music's tempo, until it suddenly stops with one forceful final *tak.* I remembered this lesson as I took a breath and began the knocking sequence, which indicated to the musicians to make the shift in music that would break the kayonan from its position of peaceful contemplation in front of my face and begin an agitated dance against the center of the screen. The gender wayang played two sequences of three beats as I touched the kayonan to the screen, the top of the puppet peeked up from the banana log, and then music and puppet united as I dragged the puppet over to the lower right side of the screen for two small, counterclockwise circles. At the top point of each circle, I paused to take a quick breath with the music before the next circle. Next, the puppet slid over to the left and repeated the same circling motion, but clockwise. After I performed this movement again, once on the right and once on the left, I lifted the kayonan away from the screen. To the audience, the movement looks as though a great gust of wind came up under the kayonan and knocked it from its place. I then swept the kayonan against the screen in large figure eights. I learned to do these figure eights even before I began practicing with the screen, because Pak Tunjung wanted to teach my body and make my muscles strong in order to gracefully execute the correct movements.

This opening dance of the kayonan demonstrates aesthetic rules that connect the performance to Balinese society and religion. Anthropologists Bruce Kapferer and Angela Hobart suggest that the consideration of aesthetics provides a means to unite art with life:

> The aesthetic and its compositional forms are what human beings are already centered within as human beings. This is to say that human beings are beings whose lived realities are already their symbolic constructions or creations within, and through which, they are oriented to their realities and come to act within them. To concentrate on the aesthetic is to focus on the dynamic forces and other processes engaged in human cultural and historical existence as quintessentially symbolic processes of continual composition and recomposition. If the aesthetic is to be equated with art, then art is life, an attention to its aesthetic processes being a concern with its compositional forms and forces in which life is shaped and comes to discover its direction and meaning. (2005, 5)

The kayonan dance thus acts as an aesthetic symbol and the practice of its use in performance demonstrates how wayang kulit makes meaning within Balinese culture.[18]

Missing from Kapferer and Hobart's use of aesthetics as an interpretive tool is the judgment that a theory of aesthetics implies; there are "good"—or within the culture, desirable—aesthetics or "bad," or undesirable, aesthetics. Bourdieu articulates how aesthetic judgment is connected to social hierarchy through his theory of taste. Bourdieu refers specifically to distinctions and comprehension of Western art, and thus not all his work is relevant; the idea, however, that understanding the art form and finding it pleasing and therefore worthwhile according to a set of established and learned rules reveals much about how wayang kulit is judged as pleasing or not pleasing and thus given a kind of tangible value within the society. If the viewer does not possess the "cultural competence" in order to understand the performance, he or she "feels lost in a chaos of sounds and rhythms, colours and lines, without rhyme or reason" (1984, 2). While in Bali, many of the foreigners I encountered expressed similar frustration with Balinese performance because they never acquired knowledge of the cultural codes and language being used in the performance. The value given the aesthetic codes also mitigates how women might be perceived and accepted as dalang.

Taksu, the primary Balinese aesthetic, describes an elusive quality that a performer or performance has in order to be judged as good, meaning that the performer pleases his or her audience and the performance is therefore deemed successful. Taksu connotes a certain spiritual connection or even age because it is something accumulated over time, and as a performer practices and gains performance experience, the performer's taksu develops. Having taksu is different from being a skilled performer—even a master might have an off night and a beginner might give a performance with strong taksu. Hobart (2003, 115) dubs taksu "the god of inspiration," which provides the dalang with the power to execute the performance. Edward Herbst calls taksu the means by which the dalang is connected to the invisible world of the spirits: "Once the shadow puppet is in the *dalang*'s grip, his hands and arms serve as a connector, a lightning rod, through which the puppet's character, voice, and spiritual life-force, *taksu,* enter the *dalang*" (1997, 61). In order for this connection to manifest and create taksu, there must be, however, a logical connection between dalang and puppet. This connection is described as *masolah,* or "characterization"— "*masolah* in its fullest meaning implies the inherent *taksu* 'spiritual energy' that integrates the state of a performer with the physical form of his own body, and/or that of a mask or puppet" (57). Pak Tunjung explained to me, "within a wayang kulit performance masolah is extremely important. It is the medium of action—the dalang must dance together with the character of the puppet. In Balinese wayang kulit, masolah provides the means for the message or meaning of the performance."

The realization of masolah, and the creation of taksu, depends on a *logical* connection between the puppet and the dalang. No connection, no taksu. Herbst describes several dalang finding difficulty with the animal characters in wayang tantri—because how can a human dalang become one with an animal character? In wayang "each character really must speak for himself, with no distance between *dalang* and puppet" (1997, 62). This creates difficulty for a woman dalang to have taksu because there is a greater social, vocal, and physical difference between her and the many male characters in the stories she performs. I had studied various styles of Asian performance while at the University of Hawai'i and often played male characters. This experience helped me greatly in bridging the gender and cultural divide between myself and the puppets I held in my hand. A male dalang can play female characters and a woman dalang can play male characters. However, it is rare to see women characters in wayang—and perhaps the greater distance between puppet and character, which is an obstacle to taksu, is why.

"Liveness" and "balance" are two additional aesthetics that are important to master for wayang kulit—the connection of masolah does not depend on voice alone. From the Balinese perspective the universe is made up of three key elements—fire, water, and air— which are constantly moving and changing. Some change is visible and some change takes place over such long periods of time that it is not readily apparent. The Balinese consider the presence of this kind of subtle movement—called *kehidupan,* or liveness—to be highly desirable within the performing arts because a static puppet or dancer appears dead. Kehidupan explains why most Balinese wayang kulit is still performed with an oil lamp even while Java and most of Southeast Asia now prefers the stronger light given by an electric lamp. The flickering flame from the oil lamp creates the appearance of constant movement and "life," even while the puppets are not moving. Pak Tunjung reminded me about the importance of my wrist; he explained that I needed to keep the kayonan in constant motion. The kayonan puppet is large but is made of thin leather that quivers with a slight wiggle of the wrist. I learned that it is important to coordinate this vibration with all the movements of the kayonan; it must look alive.

The ideal of balance, or the existence of two opposite yet complementary halves composing a whole, is a pervasive and long-standing foundation for Balinese culture and cosmology. Davies (2007, 21) asserts that balance is the primary criterion for judging whether something is beautiful, pleasing, or good—or in Balinese, *becik.* Balance in Balinese art forms is not just a matter of symmetry; it also depends on how the proportions relate back to both the human body and the cosmological configuration of the island. Balance, rather than finding expression through opposites, also recognizes a middle position between the two extremes, and much of Balinese ritual and performance strives to bring these extremes together in equilibrium. For example, temples are placed and designed in orientation to the ocean, mountains, and cardinal directions, linking sacred elements through position and proportion (James 1973, 145–48).

Balance can be expressed through gender within Balinese performance. Many elements of a performance can be coded as masculine or feminine, such as different pairs of instruments or specific types of movements. A performance can also find balance within the gender of the performers or characters. The aesthetic realization of balance within the puppets is best understood within the categories of *alus* and *kasar*. *Alus* roughly translates as refined, and *kasar* is unrefined (fig. 2.4). Many different features of the puppets communicate the personality of their characters to the audience.[19] Characteristics of an alus puppet include a smaller, slim body, a head that is tilted downward, small or narrow eyes, a small mouth, and a small nose. The puppet's kinesthetic sphere of movement will also be smaller and more delicate. A kasar puppet is often much larger, has big, bulging eyes, a large open mouth with teeth or a tongue showing (or both), is looking straight ahead or upward, and has a wide stance. Kasar puppets move much more vigorously on the screen with large sweeping motions. Vocal qualities also follow the

Figure 2.4. The characters of Momosimoko (*left*) and Arjuna (*right*) demonstrate the difference between kasar and alus. *Photo by author; puppets by I Wayan Tunjung.*

physical characteristics of the puppets. For example a kasar ogre would have a very rough, loud, and deep voice, while an alus god or hero would have a higher pitched, rhythmically slow, smooth, and melodic voice.

Many different features of the puppets communicate the personality of their characters to the audience. In his dissertation on Javanese wayang kulit, Jan Mrázek (1998) analyzes the wayang character as if it were a map because important details such as the face are crafted on a larger scale to provide greater detail.[20] Similarly, a map of a state often includes a blowup of important cities to show individual streets and landmarks. The dimensions of profile as well as their forward-facing position are mixed to contain as many details of the character as possible. The audience sees both shoulders, a side view of the head, both legs and arms, but the rest of the body is in profile. Within the categories of alus and kasar, the features can be mixed and matched and there are many shades of possibility in between the two poles. One feature cannot be read by itself but only in combination with all other features. The stylistic iconography is born out of practicality—there is a conscious effort to communicate with the audience as completely as possible.

In Bali, however, gender connects to the available range of refinement; for example, an ogre would be kasar and a prince would be alus. Most women characters are limited to alus. In casting, women often play refined male roles in dance dramas and men monopolize the kasar ones. The scale of alus and kasar suggests why I was able to study and perform wayang kulit in Bali with little obstacle. I am female and often strove to act according to the codes of conduct for women in Bali (I dressed conservatively, did not drink alcohol in public, did not smoke, and so on). As a foreigner, however, I also had greater opportunity to occupy a kasar place and to effectively perform those characters. For example, most Balinese undergo teeth filing "to distance themselves further from the fanged animal world" (Emigh and Hunt 1992, 204). I had not undergone such a ceremony. A Balinese woman as dalang risked disharmony with the characters of the puppets according to the precepts of alus and kasar, a danger that I, as a foreigner, did not share.

Within Balinese philosophy there is the idea of *"Tat twan asi,"* or "Thou art that," meaning "that every individual potentially contains within himself or herself the entire universe" (Emigh and Hunt 1992, 203). In wayang, the kayonan dance demonstrates balance between the different dimensions of the universe as it moves around the screen. The body of the dalang begins the performance by connecting to the physical and invisible worlds; enacting balance through motion. Movements on the left are matched with movements on the right, and there is also balance in how the kayonan moves between the top and the bottom of the screen. Pak Tunjung often adjusted my hand in order to facilitate this balance; I did not automatically create the same movement on the right and left but had to practice it again and again. When I first learned this section, often on the right side, the tip of the kayonan tended to slip too far down while on the left it stood up too straight. The next important motion of the kayonan dance I learned was to spin the puppet in the palm of my hand. Pak Tunjung demonstrated how I needed to set the point of the stick in the center of my palm while wrapping my fingers around the upper part of the stick. I needed to balance the kayonan in my right hand while using my fingers to make it twirl off toward the sides of the stage. During this twirling, I again used the cepala in my left hand to knock against the puppet box. All these elements needed to work together.

Most of my lessons were during the day, without an oil lamp. Finally, when we rehearsed with the lamp, I had to again learn how to adjust my body to complete the motions with something hanging directly in front of my face (fig. 2.5). I found that I needed to watch both the puppet in motion and the shadow being created on the screen. Twirling the kayonan near the lamp forced me to be aware of my body in relation to the puppet in a new way. The puppet's motions were no longer just about the motions; I now needed to watch the result of those motions, and the shadow was the visible result of the invisible intention that resided in my body.

Figure 2.5. The oil lamp hangs in front of the dalang's face. *Photo by author.*

As the dance of the kayonan is completed, the dalang and his assistants take out the rest of the puppets from the box and put them into their places around the stage. There is another section of the kayonan dancing before the puppet characters enter the scene and begin the story. The entrance of the puppets is called Alas Arum and is accompanied by music and a song. The length of the song can be adjusted depending on the number of characters entering. The version that Pak Tunjung taught me for Arjuna Tapa is:

Alas Arum

rahina tatas kemantian humuni

Every morning the gamelan music begins to play.

mredanga kala sangka gurnitan tara

The voices of the instruments are beautiful to hear.

gumuruh ikang gubar bala samuha

The sound of the crashing cymbals brings everyone together.

(*Arjuna enters.*)

Mangkata pada nguwuh seruh rumuhun

And the one with the thunderous voice progresses to the front of the line.

(*Arjuna ties his sash and fixes his crown.*)

Para ratu sampun ahyas asalin

The kings change into their grand clothes.

(*Twalen enters.*)

Lumanpaha pada hawan rata parimita

He that drives the chariot is without compare.

(*Merdah enters.*)

Arjuna is the first character to enter from the dalang's right. Pak Tunjung demonstrated how I must combine singing, the motion of the puppet, and the percussion of the cepala in this short sequence. He taught me this section by taking my hand and allowing me to feel the movements in my body; he wanted me to sense the tension of the puppet on the screen. When Arjuna stopped moving, Pak Tunjung pressed down on my hand, pushing the Arjuna puppet into the screen, and then quickly he relaxed the pressure. Next he tilted my hand in order to make Arjuna look down. "Arjuna is looking at the place around him," explained Pak Tunjung, "he is acknowledging the world that he has entered into." Arjuna then slowly moved counterclockwise, to the right side of the screen. The characters who are the heroes of the story often enter and are placed on the side of the screen to the dalang's right, while the left side is preferred for the villains of the story. When Arjuna reached the correct place, I stuck the sharp stick of the puppet into the banana log.

Next, I took the puppets for Twalen and Merdah and had them enter next and take positions on the left side of the screen, facing Arjuna. Twalen entered first; the puppet was in my hand, but he began to act as his own character. Sitting in front of the screen I was at once aware that I was controlling the puppets, but as they became more comfortable in my hand, I was less aware. The puppets became characters in a drama that moved from my mind to the screen—that is the "becoming one," or menyatu, which means that the movements of the dalang and the puppets work together so that there is no longer a barrier between them. I find that menyatu surfaces even as I write about the movements of the puppets on the screen. I keep wanting to attribute the action of the play directly to the character, and it requires careful focus to describe my movements that then result in the movements of the puppet.

The motions of the puppets indicate status between characters that are expressed within the body of the puppet and within the characters' relationships together on the screen. Twalen appeared briefly behind Arjuna before I lifted him off the screen and then placed him center. Pak Tunjung explained it was important that the head of Twalen was always lower than Arjuna's head. After crossing to the center, Twalen faced away from Arjuna, and I learned how to turn my wrist to rotate the puppet around to face Arjuna. In a performance, when a puppet changes direction, it is important to keep the face resting on the screen; therefore, a puppet always turns in, and the nose never is lifted from the screen. Pak Tunjung taught me how to dip my arm so that the puppet made a fluid motion on the screen while turning. Next I took both of Twalen's arm sticks into my right hand, lifted his arms up as Twalen bowed to Arjuna, and then returned Twalen to a standing position. Twalen then walked backward into his position on the left side of the screen; when he walks backward, his arms bend at the elbows and move back and forth, indicating motion. Pak Tunjung often had to adjust my fingers so that I gripped the sticks properly in order to make each arm move at the same time but in opposite directions. It was difficult for him to explain the instructions with words; again, the knowledge had to be passed from body to body. At home I practiced this motion with both Twalen and Merdah until I could do these different actions without thinking. I had to practice in order to join my body together with the body of the puppet without conscious effort: this is menyatu. After I had mastered the voice and movements of the penasar Twalen, Pak Tunjung told me that my puppet was just the right size for me to use and that I should not get a larger one or my voice and movements would not balance.

Arjuna's entrance was at a point in the story where the addition of the oil lamp caused me to be very aware of my own body. As Arjuna rotated backward against the screen, I learned to lift his feet further from the screen at the high points of the rotation in order to prevent the puppet from looking like he was flying above the bottom of the screen. I now needed to watch the shadow of the puppet together with the actual puppet. In a performance, after Arjuna is positioned, the dalang takes the sticks of the arms so that Arjuna can adjust the sash around his waist and adjust his crown. In my own performance, these movements were coordinated with the knocking of the cepala held between my toes. Overall, it is important for the dalang to handle the puppet so that his hands and arms do not cast shadows on the screen, and it was difficult for me to find the correct position for my hands when Arjuna fixed his crown. Foley describes her own experience performing the opening of Sudanese wayang golek: "The breath and ideas of my teacher and his teacher, and his teacher's teacher, come to life through me. Those teachers are the dalang, obscured by the screen, having passed a border of life to death. I am the wayang moving via their power" (2002, 87). Likewise, in these opening moments I am invisible, only the wayang appear on the screen; past and present are merged within these shadows.

After the puppets enter, there is a stop in the action because before the dalang continues, he must thank the gods and beg forgiveness for any errors in the performance. This section is called Penyacah Parwa:

Penyacah Parwa

Dadyata Pi . . . Ra. Tihwa. Ta pira.
Caritanan, kunang pwa samangke.

Once upon a time, it is not even known how long ago,

Yata. Ri pajangkepaneru. Sang hang asta dasa parwa.

the eighteen Parwas were composed,

Yata riniket. De rsi Kresna dwipayana.

by the holy man Kresna Dwipayana.

Mijil. Sanghyang ringgit amlah cara.

In them appears the sacred shadow figure,

Kadi gelap kumerasah—Anusuping rangdu praja mandala.

like a sheet of lightning penetrating the entire cosmos.

Yata mijil niro. Sang hyang suniantara. Amunggel punang carita.

Then suddenly appears the mighty lord of poetry to create
the story.

The next section introduces the specific story that will be told in
the performance:

Warnanan ariwijil . . . nira. Sang nararya partha.

Now Arjuna enters,

Agendurasa lawan caraka maka rwa

to discuss with his two servants,

Agya lumawada anangun tapa haneng Indra Kila Giri.

that he desires to go to the mountain, Indra Kila Giri, in
order to meditate.

Yata ni mitanian wawang anginyim nadak abawarasa
sanang . . . kana.

That is why they meet together here.

Until this point, my concentration had been primarily on the body and not the voice. Even though Alas Arum is sung, the focus is on making the voice like the kayonan; the voice must match the movement of the music, and then transfer that connection to the puppets on the screen. In this way, the dalang is not really speaking for himself but rather representing and speaking through history.

Matching my voice to the music was not the same as following a melody or hitting the right note and tempo. Balinese music does not have separate melody and harmony; rather, it is two equally balanced parts playing in counterpoint. These two parts are called *polos* and *sangsih*. The music for most wayang kulit is played on two pair of gender wayang and thus requires a two-handed technique where the musician strikes the keys with a mallet, playing both polos and sangsih, while dampening the previous notes with the sides of his hand and wrist. The instruments are deliberately tuned so that one is high and one is low, creating a "shimmering effect" in the music that perhaps sounds dissonant to Western ears (Heimarck 2003, 255–56). I learned to listen to the music and perhaps match a key note and then to sing in counterpoint to the notes being played. I found that I needed to think of balancing my voice to the music rather than singing along with the music.

Kehidupan also materializes through the voice. One way is that the voice must be clearly connected to the puppet, as I discussed above. The second quality of liveness in the voice is less tangible, but refers to the vocal prowess of the dalang. Herbst says that a standard quality of the dalang's voice is its *suara ncah*—a "broken, shattered, or fragmented" quality that often sounds very coarse or somewhat hoarse (1997, 25). When I studied this quality I found that suara ncah requires the dalang to be simultaneously relaxed while also pushing the voice. The throat is the focal point for the sound but the voice must also resonate throughout the entire body. Penyacah Parwa provides a means for warming up the suara ncah together with other pitches and vocal qualities that range from rough to sweet. A good dalang has control of this voice that is "embodying, conveying character and spirit that it's a gestural voice, shaping sounds and phrases not so much melodically as in deep sweeps of feeling" (Herbst 1997, 26). Suara ncah indicates to the audience that the dalang has taksu. In Penyacah Parwa, I was waking up *my* voice and discovering the voices of the characters that would appear in the story. The structure of the performance and meeting with people before the performance meant the dalang could not take a separate moment to warm up his voice—the Penyacah Parwa was the warmup. Each day I found that my voice was a little different. Sometimes it was pitched high and sometimes low; sometimes it was strong, sometimes weak; the sound of my voice depended on many things like the weather or what I might have eaten. The voice is not only a demonstration of skill, as I discussed earlier, but also another step in the process of menyatu, or of expressing taksu; the dalang embodies the characters in voice and action. Pak Tunjung explained that it was important to perform the opening well, otherwise the audience might judge the dalang as "not good" and go home.

After Penyacah Parwa, the dalang finally gives voice to the puppet characters. Twalen comes forward and bows to Arjuna, first asking for his blessing, before inquiring why Arjuna brought them to this place. In this scene Twalen is worried because Arjuna looks unhappy and pensive, and Arjuna responds in Kawi—the audience typically does not understand these words, but Twalen and Merdah will explain:

> *Uduh, ceraka makerua.*
> *Tanlen kaginucara kaya mangk-e.*
> *Ulun arep anangun tapa,*
> *haneng Indrakila Giri.*

> (Arjuna gestures over his shoulder as he says the name of the mountain.)

> *Moga-Moga—Raharje ikanang jagat kabeh.*
> *Mangkana pamurwaning kunang cerita.*

Merdah comes forward to the center of the screen to explain that Arjuna said he wants to go up the mountain to meditate and gain wisdom from the gods. Merdah adds that he thinks it is a very good idea, and that he and Twalen will make the journey with Arjuna. Next, Arjuna exits and leaves Twalen and Merdah to talk about the upcoming journey. Twalen expresses concern about food, where they will sleep, and encountering frightening animals. Their conversation is about the scene, but it also provides the dalang an opportunity to teach the audience things about politics or philosophy. The dialogue is not set, and I had a great deal of freedom to improvise and experiment with the content and execution of this scene.

The opening of the story is very different from the scene between the two penasar, Twalen and Merdah. Pak Tunjung wanted me to be very precise in my movements and speech and would often stop me to demonstrate a small movement of the puppet or because he wanted me to adjust my pronunciation. This part of the "tradition" is fixed, and the opening must be executed exactly the same for every performance. The opening sections of the story only take thirty minutes in a performance that might last for two or three hours, but Pak Tunjung devoted more than half our lessons to those details because they provide the foundation of the performance.

Part Two — Comedy

It is not easy to learn how to be funny. In the film *Shadow Master* (2008), about a family of Balinese dalang in the regency of Tabanan, the older teacher comments to his student, "the comedy is the hardest part; you can't teach someone to be funny. You must feel it in your heart." Likewise, during these lessons, Pak Tunjung said it is important for me to feel the characters and that they must become part of me in order to perform them. He explained that the expression of the character comes from my spirit and heart. Pak Tunjung taught me by example, but told me I would need to make it my own.

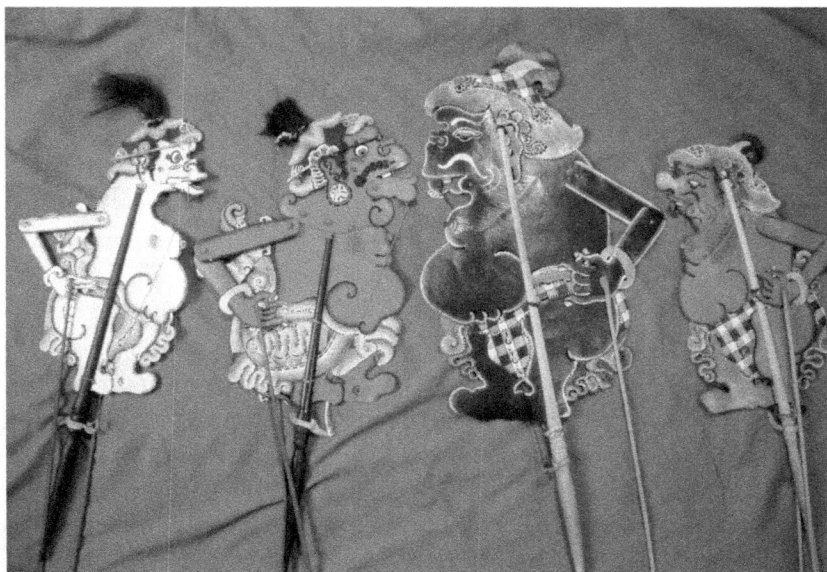

Figure 2.6. The penasar, or clown characters: (*from left*) Sangut, Delem, Twalen, and Merdah. *Photo by author; puppets by I Wayan Tunjung.*

The second section of the play begins with Delem singing and dancing vigorously around the screen. Delem, and his younger brother, Sangut (fig. 2.6), are the penasar who are featured in the second part of the story, and they are servants to the Korawas. Delem's voice can be heard even before he appears, "Ritelas hira matingkah." The rough sound of his voice is more important than the meaning of the words. While the music keeps playing, Delem can stop in the center of the screen in order to fix his hair. "Slowly, slowly," Pak Tunjung would remind me—these actions demonstrate the vain disposition of Delem's character. Delem is the larger and more robust of the two brothers and he has reddish-brown skin. He has rather grand-looking clothes and acts like a rich man even though he is poor; he is rather pompous and self-important. His voice is rough and gravelly and it comes from the throat. His hair, made from cow's hair, is thick and it often bounces because his movements are very fast to indicate his rash personality.

Delem functions as a huge contrast to his brother Sangut, who is shorter, thinner, and has long, unkempt hair with a high-pitched, nasal voice. Sangut is poor and slow but is also the more humble and thoughtful of the two. I would make Delem's arm spin around on its axis so that it looked like the puppet was running his fingers through his hair. Pulling his mouth slightly open, I would then quickly turn him to face right and then left, as if Delem was smiling at the audience and asking for approval. Then, as if he decided his hair was not properly combed, he would spit into his hand and again run his fingers through his hair. Pak Tunjung demonstrated by making a very loud sound, like gagging and snorting, as the puppet's hand rested near its mouth. The action would repeat several times, each time the sound of spitting and snorting would be louder and grosser. Finally Delem sighed, "Ahhhh . . . ," and resumed dancing to the music. The music only stopped as Delem began to holler for his brother to hurry up and come join him on the screen. "Sanguuut! Ngut Ngut Ngut! Come here, here, here!" I was taught to have the puppet call out. Sangut entered from the left of the screen in order to dialogue with Delem. Together these two characters provide the richest range of comedy and social commentary within a play:

> DELEM: My brother, why are you so late in coming here? Where were you?
>
> SANGUT: Oh, I am so sorry—I needed to sleep in this morning. I was finally able to sleep well.
>
> DELEM: What do you mean?
>
> SANGUT: Well, last night there was a great deal of noise coming from the courtyard, all night long. And I looked out my window to see that it was you—singing and dancing.
>
> DELEM: Oh?
>
> SANGUT: But your dancing looked like a sick dog in the road. Balinese dancers have special movements

and ways of doing things. If you do not know the correct movements, the musicians will not be able to follow. It is important to do the dance correctly to honor the gods.

DELEM: Bah! What do you know?!? I think you are just lazy, sleeping in like that.

SANGUT: OK, Brother, whatever you say.

In this scene Delem and Sangut comment on the maintenance of tradition in Bali; artists must strive for a level of excellence in their dance to balance with the music. Many Balinese feel that the last decade saw horrible consequences with the tragedy of the Bali bombs when the arts were not performed in honor of the gods. The dialogue between the clowns indicates how important the proper performance of tradition through the arts is to honor the gods and maintain social harmony.

Unlike the first scene, where the penasar Twalen and Merdah function in service to the action of the main characters, Delem and Sangut dominate their part of the story. This demonstrates a shift from aesthetic concerns, which connect the world of the play to the spiritual realm, to a preoccupation with the immediate material context of the play. Rather than preach religious philosophy, Delem and Sangut debate political matters or argue about local gossip. Within this context, the dalang is excused from social and political frameworks that might otherwise limit speech concerning controversial topics. The first part of the play establishes a godly authority, Twalen is often said to have descended from the gods (Hobart 1985, 48) and he with his son Merdah translate the words of the refined characters for the audience. The second part uses the comedy of Delem and Sangut in order to demonstrate power within the context of the earthly realm.

Delem and Sangut often break social rules through their dialogue and actions. Hobart describes a scene where the penasar accused a local woman of witchcraft, because she was publically exposed her magic could no longer carry any power. This exchange was only possible because of the freedom allowed the dalang through these characters—in life the Balinese would hesitate to ever call someone a witch (Hobart 1985, 47). Likewise, the Balinese would also be reluctant to criticize someone's dancing. There are many reasons why the dalang is afforded such a special status in Balinese performance, but the primary one I am concerned with here is the use of comedy as a unique vehicle of social criticism. Ron Jenkins explains: "*Penasar* is the Balinese word for foundation, and their title indicates the fundamental role of clowns in the temple performances" (1994, 20). Fredrik deBoer defines the term as "basic characters" (1987, 79). Through learning how to create comic scenes with Delem and Sangut, I was able to participate within the foundations of the Balinese social sphere.

Social life in Bali is based around gender and community. Like many other women students studying traditional performance in Bali—I only had access to male teachers (Palermo 2007, 226). Women must therefore negotiate physical and social differences in order to learn and perform wayang kulit. The history of the women's movement throughout Indonesia can be understood as an attempt to gain influence within the public sphere rather than the private sphere of the home. Luh Ketut Suryani, a Balinese scholar, writes, "In Bali, the primary female role is one of fostering balance and harmony within families." Women are expected to marry, produce children, and "work as part of a family team," and much of that teamwork is the making of offerings, both simple and elaborate, to be used in daily or special ceremonies (2004, 213). Ni Made Wiratini, a Balinese scholar who teaches at ISI, argues that Balinese women represent a kind of "wonder woman" because they have three different roles in society: "a domestic role (housekeeping), a public/economic role (earning money), and a social role (traditional duties). The social role is the most important and it cannot be ignored because it is related to ceremonial duties" (2009, 31).[21] Wiratini argues that women are taking over the responsibility for preserving tradition, often as expressed through the arts, within

Balinese culture. She researched women dancers in the area around Denpasar and argues that the reason those women want to perform and work as artists is to perpetuate their culture. The women Wiratini interviewed saw the practice of traditional arts as vital to the maintenance of their identity as Balinese, but the women did not equate participation in the arts with having greater power in the social sphere. Women's involvement seems to indicate that some of the arts are moving into the shadows, or domestic sphere, rather than women moving meaningfully into the public sphere.

Delem and Sangut require the dalang to engage in the public sphere—the dalang negotiates both public and private in these popular scenes. The penasar act boldly, say what is on their mind, and do not at all personify the deferential and often *malu,* or shy, personality of the Balinese, especially women. Wiratini describes women's prescribed behavior, or *etika,* in Bali: "She has to be polite, gentle, refined, and those who do not follow those unspoken rules are considered not normal" (quoted in Palermo 2007, 233). The penasar are difficult for any dalang—but especially difficult for a woman dalang.

Delem and Sangut occupy a special status and provide the dalang with an opportunity to demonstrate his taksu. Hobart writes that in their outspoken role these two clowns mediate conflict, acting as "orators" within the village council who "predominate and influence." The penasar represent the public, giving the impression of equality even as they reinforce the hierarchy of the society (Hobart 1985, 48). This is similar to how Jane Goodall describes the actor during the Renaissance in England: "In metaphysical terms, the actor was an equalizer, a channel for presence and authority of many kinds but also someone in whom the condition of human morality was epitomized"; the actor represents the lowest dregs of humanity while also realizing a potential for greatness (2008, 52). Likewise the penasar not only represent the lowest levels of society, because they are servants of the lowest caste, but they also have unique political and spiritual power that positions them among the highest levels of society. Although contemporary Bali offers a very different context than the one that inspired Goodall, the reasons she gives for the power of the English actor proves useful for understanding how the similar status and privilege of Delem and Sangut function.

Goodall locates the power of the actor in the actor's genius, attraction or magnetism, and the ability to move. Genius suggests both great knowledge and exceptional inspiration that results in the ability to draw vast audiences to the stage. Goodall (2008, 57–59) cites Kant in order to define artistic genius as a quality that cannot be taught because the artist himself cannot articulate or teach his method for creativity. These comments resonate with the ideas shared at the beginning of this section—comedy cannot be taught. Pak Tunjung implored me to practice with these characters at home in order to invest their personalities in my soul. I discovered, like the dalang who chats with his sponsor before the performance to learn the local gossip, that the best way to prepare to perform with the penasar was to read the newspaper and talk with others about what was trendy or important at the moment of my performance. A dalang uses his genius, or inspiration, in performance to attract audiences that number in the hundreds or even thousands. The performance is for the gods, but many dalang will comment about the energy they receive from the human audience and boast about the numbers who gather to watch their performance. A Balinese woman would struggle to have the freedom to practice an art daily because of her many duties to family and community. Time and social constraints limit the "genius" that a woman might be able to achieve in her performance.

The power of attraction suggests that artistic genius can result in a type of physical force or power, like gravity, that the performer can use to draw attention to himself (Goodall 2008, 61). Like taksu, magnetic attraction allows the performer to possess an indescribable power, one, as Goodall (62) explains, that is almost "magical" in its effect. Through the clowns, the dalang demands the attention of the audience. I have observed conversations hush and people gather closer around the screen during these comic scenes as if pulled there by some invisible force.

The clowns might manipulate the audience, but are they able to manipulate and change society? The actions of an actor with this kind of stage presence, an actor that possesses artistic genius and the power of attraction, manifests itself physically and emotionally in the audience. "Somehow the singular presence of the actor on the stage had an impact upon the massed people in the audience. The reactive effects were palpable: from the social reactions of laughter and applause through to the deeper physiological sympathy that caused tears to flow, or the spectator's blood to run cold when the actor encountered a ghost" (Goodall 2008, 66). In Bali, laughter is among the greatest effective powers that a dalang can invoke in his audience. Jenkins describes how the antics of the clown[22] within a ceremonial performance were able to defuse possibly volatile situations, whether they involved tourists interrupting the ceremony or an unplanned visit by the governor of Bali. In each case, "the power of Balinese temple clowns is rooted in the social complexity of the laughter they evoke. Their comedy is both subversive and cohesive. They mockingly subvert the destructive potential of Western development at the same time that they reinforce the spiritual and cultural bonds that make their audience a community" (1994, 43). Jenkins argues that laughter makes the clowns subversive; however, I would say that this power is more limited. While the clowns do speak out and act against outside powers, such as Westernization and to a lesser extent national concerns, in the end, the performance uses the presence of the comic characters to reinforce the habitus of the Balinese community. Laughter is the practice that ties people to their social structures, and a young dalang must practice comedy in order to make people laugh. The comedy, rather than challenging hegemony in a meaningful way, provides the kind of release that Mikhail Bakhtin (1998, 251) suggests in his writings on carnival— the world is turned upside down, but at the end of the performance, it must be returned. The regular social structures are reinforced because they were given a space and time for release.

Like the characters Delem and Sangut, women dalang reinforce, rather than challenge, social hegemony. Carmencita Palermo cites

I Wayan Dibia, a Balinese artist and scholar, who feels that women should explore performance opportunities within male forms— but in doing so they should not stop "acting like a woman":

> [Dibia] believes that women should choose stories with female characters by modifying the characters of topeng, or by creating new characters and new masks. He is particularly intense about the penasar characterised by a woman. In order to characterise that mask a woman has to force herself to move, walk like a man and wear trousers; this is considered by Dibia as not following the "etika," it is not proper. In order to avoid this abuse and succeed in the characterisation, it is necessary to suit the mask to the woman's natural character. (2007, 237)

Women are not able to achieve masolah, or balance, with the characters of Delem and Sangut. Dibia suggests that women should develop their own characters and style—but a wayang performance without the iconic characters Delem and Sangut would have little power and perhaps little audience.

After a while, the dialogue between Delem and Sangut turned to the main focus of the scene. In performance I had seen dalang take almost thirty minutes with their first exchange, discussing many different subjects such as education, health care, or traffic jams. Finally, in the story I learned, Delem tells Sangut that their boss, Momosimoko, wants them to help him kill Arjuna. At first, Sangut is horrified by the idea and explains that he does not think Arjuna did anything wrong. Delem tells Sangut that Arjuna must die because he is praying for favors from the gods and might receive a big weapon or, even worse, the hand in marriage of a beautiful heavenly princess. Sangut sighs and admits that he has no choice but to follow the orders of Momosimoko. The conversation between the clowns suggests the wisdom of the lower castes, the common people, as Sangut longs for justice, but at the end of the scene hierarchy is restored. Momosimoko outranks his servants and they must follow his orders, even if they do not agree. Through the characters Delem and Sangut, the dalang both acts upon and maintains the basic structures of society. The "wisdom" shared serves, rather than subverts, the greater social order. The aesthetic of balance is both upset and reinforced within the actions and comedy of the characters.

Part Three — Receptions

A famous Balinese proverb is, "Like war in the shadow play." This proverb describes a man and woman who fight and argue during the day but then sleep quietly together in the same bed at night. "The analogy is taken from the puppets who are thought of as sleeping in their box, out of sight of the public, and who only come to life when they fight, and so more generally when they are seen on the stage. It is only then that the nexus which binds individuals and groups with one another is illustrated" (Hobart 1985, 53). Conflict, especially war and battle, are among the most important moments of the play. The third section always includes dynamic fighting among many different puppets and is therefore the realization of the struggle building within the first two sections of the play. At the end of the battle, cosmic balance is restored, the performance ends, and the puppets are stored together in the box until they are needed for another performance.

Even though the battle scenes depict great conflict, the key to performing these complex scenes is in coordinating many different parts of the body to work together. Pak Tunjung began to teach me the movements for fighting by having me hold Arjuna in one hand and Momosimoko in the other hand. He instructed me to begin with the puppets facing each other and then as I hammered the cepala against the box with my left foot in a burst of percussion, the puppets each would dip down as if they were taking a good look at one another. Pak Tunjung explained that the initial fighting movement was not so difficult, but required stamina from the dalang, who had already been performing for several hours. As the cepala knocked a rhythm against the box the puppets would cross in front of each other, turn, and cross again. The movement, though simple, looked vigorous and powerful to the audience watching on the other side of the screen. Pak Tunjung demonstrated several different ways I could show the puppets doing battle: one puppet could throw another, jump on the adversary's head, shoot an arrow, or many other amazing possibilities.

Often many different puppets might appear from different directions in order to fight, requiring the dalang to maintain coordination and balance both on the screen in view of the audience and off the screen as he exchanges puppets and weapons. Learning this process is where my own practice became distinct from the watchful eye of my teacher; it was a test of the techniques and aesthetics he had taught me. One day, I arrived at Pak Tunjung's house for my lesson, but he was not there, so I sat and waited for a few minutes and then decided to move over to the screen to practice by myself. It was really useful to rehearse the manipulation of the puppets with the screen, and I practiced the details of moving my hands in conjunction with the voices. I set the puppets in their positions on the screen and practiced picking each one up, having him walk across the screen, and then repositioning him again before I let go. Pak Tunjung had explained that it was important for the puppets to "stand" leaning slightly forward as to look "alive." If the puppet leaned too far forward it looked like it might fall on its nose, and if it leaned too far back Pak Tunjung complained that the puppet looked like "it will fall backwards, dead." I repeated the motions many times so that the proper positions might become ingrained into my body. Sometimes I grasped the puppet on the right with my left hand and then realized that I was in a poor position to grab the puppet on the left with my right hand, my arms twisted like pretzels as I tried to bring both the puppets to the screen. Finally I had to admit failure, set the puppets down, and try the scene again. I needed to remember to hold the puppets on the right with my right hand and the ones on the left with my left hand, and to anticipate which hand would need to be free for the next puppet. I had only three puppets on the screen, but the combinations appeared endless as I sorted through the correct movements to connect my body to the body of the puppet.

After I practiced the opening movements, I skipped to the end of the performance in order to practice the fight scenes. I took Arjuna in my left hand and the raksasa, or ogre, in the right and practiced crossing them in front of me to the steady beat of the cepala from my foot. The puppets needed to cross the front of the screen at the same time, and then on the next beat turn to face each other before crossing the scene once again. If the raksasa crossed in front on the way over, the same puppet needed to be in the front on the way back. It was important to hold the puppets close to the screen, but if I held them too close they would become twisted and stick together. The puppets and my body swung together in motion; it was a dance that engaged my person from head to toe. After only a minute of this sequence I was covered in sweat and breathing hard, but I paused only a moment to catch my breath before I resumed the sweeping dance across the screen. After practicing this basic fighting movement I also rehearsed another sequence in which Arjuna hits the raksasa and knocks him over. Each beat of this sequence needs to be punctuated with a tak, as the puppets grapple across the screen. As I practiced, the other family members in the compound were busy cleaning, preparing food, and making offerings. I rehearsed alone for several hours and then waved goodbye to the family. I learned later that Pak Tunjung had gone to take his wife to Denpasar so she could fly to Jakarta for a conference. The time alone at the screen provided me with strength and confidence in performance. I depended on Pak Tunjung to transfer the knowledge of wayang from his body to mine, but I must also practice alone in order for that knowledge to be really present within my body.

Pak Tunjung sometimes experienced censure from others in the village because he was teaching me wayang kulit. One day, while we worked on carving puppets, a man I had never seen before, dressed in pakian adat, came to speak with Pak Tunjung. After the two spoke a moment in Balinese, Pak Tunjung turned to me and explained in English that he had told the man I was only there to learn a little about wayang kulit. The man glared at me and I did not speak to him. From the way Pak Tunjung spoke to me in English I felt that perhaps I should not reveal my ability to speak Indonesian, or try to get into a conversation with the stranger. He made me uneasy because I had the impression he had stopped by to check up on Pak Tunjung. Finally the man left and we did not talk about the encounter but continued to work on the puppets. I worried that Pak Tunjung might be receiving criticism from others in the village because he was teaching wayang kulit to a foreign woman. I did not see this as a reluctance to share Balinese culture as much as envy over money and privilege. Foreigners are able to pay for music and dance lessons, while many Balinese cannot; teaching foreigners is therefore a good income source and often provides the teacher with a greater degree of respect within the community. This opens the door for others to feel envious, and it is possible that this envy might be more keenly expressed in this case because it is very rare for a foreigner, especially a woman, to learn wayang kulit. The actions of both teacher and student reverberate throughout the Balinese community.

Learning how to balance the conflict happening on the screen with the coordination in my body describes the process by which the student dalang must both reflect the values and skill of his teacher and innovations that make him or her unique. About eight months into my training, Pak Tunjung told me that I Nyoman Sedana, a professor at the university, had asked him, "Can Jennifer already play wayang?" Pak Tunjung told him, "Yes, Jennifer can." He said that Pak Sedana was surprised that I was an American and could already perform wayang kulit. Pak Sedana said he hoped that people would watch my performance and realize that Pak Tunjung had an American student who was already good at performing. Pak Tunjung emphasized that it was important for me to do a good job in my performance so that others would think well of him, because people often judge a teacher based on the performance of his student.

Foley explains, "If a teacher teaches wrongly, it can cause dispersal of his or her own store of spiritual power, or, even worse, sickness or bad luck" (1990, 77). During a few difficult rehearsals I learned that my own performance related back to Pak Tunjung's reputation and power within Balinese society. After a rehearsal for Pak Tunjung's family and some friends from the village, I stayed behind after everyone left so that Pak Tunjung could give me some notes on my performance. He told me to be careful not to bring the puppets too close to each other in the center of the screen because it looked like they were kissing. Instead, I should use the oil lamp as a marker for the center and have the puppets on either side of center. Finally, he bid me goodnight and we agreed to meet the next day for another rehearsal at night. It would be without the musicians, but Pak Tunjung wanted me to practice again with the oil lamp.

The next day I took a painting class that lasted most of the day and was quite tired before getting to Pak Tunjung's for rehearsal. That rehearsal did not go well; I did not have much energy and I kept making mistakes. Near the end, Pak Tunjung interrupted me and complained that I was doing it all wrong. He then demonstrated for me what he wanted and added some new dialogue. I felt frustrated because he was describing things that were completely new, and Pak Tunjung was very upset and not very patient. He told me that the opening was not very good because it lacked energy, and he scolded me because I was not holding Delem the correct way when the puppet was dancing. He told me that if I did the performance like that he would feel very *malu* (shy and embarrassed). His words felt extremely harsh. Before I left, he said we should meet early the next day to rehearse. I went home feeling very sad, and wondered if there was any way out of my commitment to do a public performance.

The next few rehearsals were not easy. Pak Tunjung told me he was worried about my performance and was not able to eat. I was frustrated because he kept changing the ending and I still was missing a couple of the puppets for an early scene. The puppets were still at the painters, and I was worried whether they would be done in time for the performance. Pak Tunjung told me not to worry, that he would lend me his puppets if mine were not finished. That made me more relaxed, but I still needed to rehearse the scenes with those puppets, and I did not have puppets for practice. Additionally, every time he changed the scene, I had more Kawi to memorize and it was difficult for me to remember the strange words. Pak Tunjung was adamant that I could not use a script, so I carried my note cards with me everywhere to try to memorize the difficult sounds. As the week progressed, slowly the details for the performance emerged, and I felt more confident about my performance. Like the puppets in the battle scenes, the actions of teacher and student coordinated and affected each other, moving in and out of balance.

After the Performance

At the end of a performance the dalang sets the kayonan at the center of the screen and, with the help of his assistants, the puppets are packed away into the box. After the box has been shut, the dalang gives final offerings to the puppets and other objects used within the performance. The screen is disassembled, the oil lamp taken down, and the sound system unplugged. The dalang steps away from the playing area to chat with his host while the musicians and assistants wander away to smoke. From the embodied moments of performance, the only thing left are the various objects—even sitting there, lifeless, they contain the power of wayang kulit.

Often after a performance someone from the audience will come and ask to have the oil left in the oil lamp after it is extinguished. The oil, by virtue of being a part of the practice of performance, is said to be endowed with restorative power. I have often seen old men rub the oil into backs or legs as an antidote for the pain. The oil is also said to work on sickness or skin diseases. Regular coconut oil would not be effective; rather, this oil from the lamp has benefited from the spiritual power of the performance. Objects, together with practice, create meaning both inside and outside the performance. Like the oil, each object interacts with the tradition of wayang kulit to have both reflective and creative power within Balinese society.

Chapter 3

OBJECTS OF TRADITION

*Wayang without a dalang have no use, a dalang
without wayang cannot find a way.*
—"Ensiklopedia mini pewayangan Bali"[1]

*Theatrical practice has always and inevitably dealt
with stuff, in all of its messiness. It engages with the
"thingness" of the material world in ways that few
other art practices do.*
—Knowles 2012, 1

Museum Bali, located adjacent to Puputan Square in Denpasar, displays cultural and historical objects "intended to appreciate our cultural inheritance as well as giving a full understanding about history of Balinese cultural development" (Bali Cultural Office 2013).[2] Within one of the museum's exhibits, the puppet figures of Duryodana and Bima (fig. 3.1) face each other as if they are ready to jump into battle—but they are motionless behind the glass at the museum. Below them the figures of the penasar, or clowns, are likewise frozen. The puppets depend on the description provided by the museum rather than the hands and voice of a dalang to give them personality and character. The sign nearby, "Wayang Parwa with Bhartayuda—War Theme of Mahabrata Epic," explains that the *lakon,* or story, is about the war between two families of first cousins, the Pandawas and the Korawas. The Korawas are described as greedy, sly, and eager to rule; in contrast the Pandawas

Figure 3.1. Wayang on display at Museum Negeri Propinsi Bali. *Photo by author.*

are pronounced noble and brave. The Pandawas are declared the eventual winners of the epic battle.

Examining the figures of these two puppets in the museum reveals how necessary the live performance is to creating distinct characters. The figure of Bima is a little larger than that of Duryodana, but in appearance they are quite similar. Each has large round eyes, each holds a fierce-looking weapon, each has a strong body, and each wears an ornate headdress. Upon just looking at the figures on display, one would not be able to determine that one puppet represented good or the other, bad. The posted information does not give the same nuance to the personalities of these characters as a dalang would in performance. Sometimes Bima acts rash and selfish and sometimes Duryodana performs deeds that are brave and noble. The collection of wayang kulit on display at the museum includes only about fifteen puppets. These few puppets are meant to represent the entire tradition and practice of wayang kulit. Numerous such exhibits in Bali and throughout Indonesia beg the questions of what value and what meaning are ascribed to the objects used in a wayang kulit beyond the context of performance.

The objects of wayang kulit complicate the often presumed nature of tradition—that it is passed down from generation to generation unchanging. Wayang kulit draws much of its own worth from the idea that it is a marker of the past and therefore contains some kind of authentic Balinese identity. Mathew Cohen, Alessandra Lopez y Royo, and Laura Noszlopy note, "Such traditionalism is at least in part a legacy of Dutch scholarship which tended to reify Indonesian performance by assuming fixedness and strict adherence to immutable rules" (2007, 1). These prejudices have been internalized by the Balinese, who often value "real" traditions and complain of modernization and globalization "ruining" Balinese performance and the culture that it represents. Museums and other attempts to preserve cultural objects, such as wayang kulit, operate as part of this system.

The exhibit at Museum Bali demonstrates the tendency for framing objects as tradition in several ways. The puppets are part of a larger exhibit in the Tabanan building, which "is reflecting south part of Balinese architecture and have been used for storing the heirlooms during the kingdom period" (Bali Cultural Office 2013). In different histories of Bali, there is no specific period that would generally be referred to as the "kingdom" period; rather, the term suggests that the building and items within it reflect a "timeless past" that predates modernity. Accordingly, the display does not indicate when the puppets were made. Nor does it tell who carved or painted the puppets or from which region they came, suggesting that the tradition of wayang kulit represents a permanence and thus a "universal" Balinese identity linked to the past. Finally, there is very little within the objects to suggest their use and meaning within either contemporary or historical Balinese society. Under the heading "Puppet Shadow Play," a sign in both Indonesian and English describes that the puppets are made of leather and painted bright colors; this description contrasts with the dark, faded colors of the puppets on display. The sign gives little information about performance practices, mentioning only that the performance is done by a dalang, "the puppet player," and is in Old Javanese (Kawi), while the servant characters translate the performance into the Balinese language. The rest of the sign is dedicated to describing the items used in a daytime performance (versus the night performance): a string, a screen, a lamp, and musicians. There are no images of people or photos of a performance; rather, the objects sit isolated on display. As James Clifford describes, within the museum exhibit, "people and things are increasingly out of place" (1988, 6).

The key objects of wayang kulit—the puppet box and the puppets themselves—function as material culture, "a phenomenon that clearly manifests personal and collective identity through objects, their construction processes and their usages" (Hulsbosch, Bedford, and Chaiklin 2009, 12). Examining how the objects are made, judged, and evolve over time reveals how wayang kulit gains power through its status as tradition, and how within that status, function contradictory notions of aesthetic judgment, artistic creativity, and the passing of knowledge and objects from person to person. As Clifford suggests, "'cultural' difference is no longer a stable, exotic otherness; self-other relations are matters of power and rhetoric rather than of essence. A whole structure of expectations about authenticity in culture and in art is thrown in doubt" (1988, 14). The objects of wayang kulit, as objects of material culture, incorporate their design, use, mythologies, and underlying social significance into the historically situated structures of Balinese society. The objects forge a relationship between the self and society that is reflected within and inscribed upon the object in gendered and hierarchical ways.

The Puppet Box: Negotiating Tradition in the Material Realm

> *Like all systems of norms, those concerning the past
> constitute a link between cultural concepts and social
> action. But unlike any other set of norms, this set is,
> necessarily, a code for societies to talk about themselves,
> and not only within themselves. This is so because the
> past is an intrinsically alternative mode of discourse to
> those other cultural modes of communication which
> can, and often do, assume an eternal present. Such
> norms, therefore, constitute an aspect of culture in
> which concessions to change are built in, and division
> and debate are recognised. As a result, such norms
> permit new forms of action, at the same time as they
> allow cultures to regulate social change.*
> —Appadurai 1981, 218

Wayang kulit requires many objects for a performance, such as
the puppets, the box in which they are kept, musical instruments,
the screen, sound system, and the oil lamp. The puppet chest is usually made out of the wood from the jackfruit tree, which is a rich
honey color or darker (fig. 3.2). The typical box is about three feet
long with a simple sliding lid. Often called the *kropak* or *gedog,* the
box offers a good example of how an object acquires meaning and
value through practice in wayang kulit because, as Pak Tunjung
told me, "In order to be a dalang, one must have a puppet box."
Often around Bali, when I mentioned that I was studying puppetry or that I was giving a wayang kulit performance, Balinese
people would ask me if I had a box. When I confirmed that I did,
they would nod that yes, I must be a dalang. Occasionally, I would
even be asked if I might perform for a ceremony at their temple
sometime. Another time Pak Tunjung said that a friend wanted
to borrow some puppets and also his box. He let the friend borrow
a few puppets but would not let him use the box, because as Pak
Tunjung explained, it was necessary to own your own box in order

Figure 3.2. The author's puppet box. *Photo by author.*

to perform. The object and its use give the dalang his status as a performer, but there is more to having a puppet box than simply owning one. A man or woman who wishes to be a dalang must own and care for his or her own puppet box.

The puppet box is an object from the past that operates within a discourse of norms that provide insight into how wayang kulit connects to social structures within Balinese society. Social theorist Arjun Appadurai offers a framework that can be generally applied in order to understand how the past—and, I assert, especially past marked as "tradition"—operates in relation to social structures. He "takes for granted that the discourse concerning the past between social groups is an aspect of politics, involving competition, opposition, and debate" (1981, 202). In order to articulate how such debates are culturally organized Appadurai proposes four constraints that act upon the normative past:

1. *Authority:* this dimension involves some cultural consensus as to the kinds of source, origin, or guarantor of "pasts" which are required for their credibility.

2. *Continuity:* involves some cultural consensus as to the nature of the linkage with the source of authority which is required for the minimal credibility of a "past."

3. *Depth:* involves cultural consensus as to the relative values of different time-depths in the mutual evaluation of "pasts" in a given society.

4. *Interdependence:* implies the necessity of some convention about how closely any past must be interdependent with other "pasts" to ensure minimal credibility. (1981, 203)

These four constraints establish a framework for the ways a puppet box functions as tradition by providing clarity when examining how a puppet box is used, made, and valued. These constraints also provide insight into obstacles facing women who wish to study wayang kulit and become dalang.

Early in my training, Pak Tunjung declared that I must have a box made, which is not a simple or quick process but demonstrates how "depth" is created through the consensus and involvement of many different people. First, Pak Tunjung wanted to find wood that was of a consistent quality and that would make a satisfying sound when struck during the performance. He consulted with wood dealers but also trusted his own knowledge and experience. After finding and buying the wood, he went to a friend who makes boxes. Pak Tunjung was uncertain about the size; he first thought that a smaller box might be easier for me, a woman, to use and transport, but he also realized that a smaller box might not fit the puppets or make a proper sound. Pak Tunjung visited his friend often while my box was being completed to make sure that the work matched his specifications. He sometimes complained that he was worried his friend would substitute wood of a poorer quality. The object's status as tradition also depended on its perceived future use; Pak Tunjung did not tell his friend that the box was being made for a foreigner—a box to be used by an outsider might not be given the same care as one to be used by a Balinese dalang. Finally, months later, I was able to use the box in rehearsal.

A puppet box is often a family heirloom passed down from generation to generation, and much of a puppet box's worth comes from the sense of continuity associated with it. As the box ages and is used, it is believed to gain taksu, or spiritual power, from each subsequent generation (Hobart 1987, 33). The older the puppet chest and the puppets contained within, the more power these items are believed by the Balinese to possess for ritual and performance. The dalang who possesses such a box is therefore given high status within Balinese society. Even though puppet boxes are often passed from one generation to the next, this is not true of all boxes. Pak Tunjung has two boxes: one is old and from his grandfather, and the other one he commissioned a few years ago. He uses both boxes for performances depending on practicality (for example, the puppets he needs for that performance are already in the box) and impact, because the newer box might look more flashy, while the older, darkly stained box possesses a greater mystique. Even so, each box gives his performance credibility and authority because of the "pastness" that is associated with this object in Balinese society.

Pak Tunjung decided he was not completely satisfied with my box nor his other newer one; he wanted them to be "special." He therefore had a friend, Pak Konrad, carve designs into the boxes. Initially, my box did not have thick enough wood around the frame for carving, so Pak Konrad carved the designs into separate pieces of wood that were later attached. The decorated boxes were often admired by spectators for their unique floral designs and how "rich" they looked. Several people offered to purchase my box before I had it shipped home to the United States, but Pak Tunjung refused and kept it for me. For the audience, how the designs marked my box as "traditional," even though the carving was a new innovation, demonstrates how tradition is a value judgment based on interdependence with other cultural ideas of "tradition" rather than a true indication of age or a connection to the past.

These boxes appeared "traditional," "rich," and "special," and that value carries over to the dalang using the box.

Authority, in the case of the box, refers both to the expertise of the person using it and to the practical usefulness of the box. Pak Tunjung said that the real value of my box was not only its fine appearance but that it made a very good sound when knocked with the cepala. The long side of the box that faces the dalang is hinged so that the side will swing loose, and when the dalang strikes it with the small hammer held between the toes, it makes a variety of sounds. If the dalang strikes the chest with the cepala only, the loose side also swings in and echoes the percussive sound, making a loud *tak-tak*. If he strikes the box with the entire surface of his foot, his heel and the cepala at once, the side swings in and reinforces the sounds of the percussion. The different options of striking the box each indicate a different cue to the musicians, thus prompting them to start or stop the music. For example, a single *tak*, where only the cepala strikes the box, indicates that a character is going to speak. The foot and cepala striking the box simultaneously, making a *blak*, ends a sequence of action. The cepala and the heel might alternate striking the box to make a quick rhythm, and these complicated patterns accompany fighting, singing, walking, and so on (Rubin and Sedana 2007, 34–35).

A box becomes more valuable with time and use, creating its own sense of continuity and depth: the quality of my box together with my ability to use it improved with time. During one lesson, while I was practicing coordinating striking the box with the cepala held in my foot while moving puppets with my hands against the screen, Pak Tunjung decided he was not satisfied with the sound. He went to get some safety pins and washers and used a safety pin to slide out the fastener that holds the swinging side of the box in place so he could adjust the number of washers holding it aloft, thus allowing it to swing. He disassembled and reassembled the box several times before he was satisfied, but finally it made a clear, loud sound. Several times during the months of my study he made similar adjustments. When I was preparing to return home, he told me that the box would work well for me in America because I was able to rehearse and perform with it in Bali. The history of activity gave the box its identity as a "good" box, which in turn reinforced my identity as a dalang.

Many of these things that make a puppet box effective as a ritual object in performance also make the box difficult for a woman to acquire. I had to depend on many other people and the guidance of Pak Tunjung to purchase my box. The system is controlled by men and access to the system requires a level of expertise. A woman dalang would not be able to negotiate it alone. A box is expensive, but I had funding from my university for my research. Women in Bali would struggle to come up with such a large sum of money—very few dalang purchase a new box. More commonly, a box is inherited, but a son or grandson would be preferred over a daughter to inherit such a spiritually powerful object.

The box demonstrates in a single example the many different forces that must be considered when examining the objects of wayang kulit as material culture to understand their relationship to the larger social sphere. One is how the object is both valued and gives value, because a dalang must have a box. Age gives the box added spiritual value, but that value is practical as well. A box is expensive and requires labor to make, which limits who can become a dalang. Rituals and ceremonies further tie the dalang to the box, making it part of not only an economic value system but also a spiritual value system. The aesthetics of the box can change, thus demonstrating the flexible nature of tradition and how the idea of "tradition" becomes part of something's value—for example, the carved flowers on my box were praised as both innovative and traditional at the same time. Puppets are kept in the box, and my analysis of the box provides the framework for how I will consider the puppets as objects.

Puppets as Objects

The puppets, called wayang or *ringgit,* are the most prominent part of Balinese wayang kulit, because they are the primary tools of the dalang for conveying the story. Some of the puppets are old and some are new, but Angela Hobart, in her book describing wayang kulit, asserts that the appearance of the puppets is unchanging and full of meaning: "The puppets are made according to a fixed scheme laid down in antiquity and sanctified by the force of tradition. This determines their forms, costume, and skin colors" (1987, 67). Hobart's description reflects general Balinese attitudes that the iconography of the puppets is "fixed" and therefore contributes to a rhetoric of "tradition" that reinforces it as timeless. My experience in Bali confirmed that there are recognizable characters and characteristics of the puppets, but that these are by no means static. Puppet carvers and dalang often experiment and add subtle, and sometimes not so subtle, variations, often in response to the changing aesthetics of the audience and in relation to how those aesthetics are understood in Balinese society.

Describing the puppets in wayang kulit as objects implies that the puppets form an aesthetic archive that through analysis can reveal certain truths about the Balinese. The puppets, however, are not a fixed text. Taylor describes this quandary when she notes two key myths about the archive that must be acknowledged as false: "One is that it is unmediated, that objects located there might mean something outside the framing apparatus of the archival impetus itself." An archive is created through a process of selection—some things are included and some things are left out. By examining how the objects of wayang kulit are made and appraised, I hope to reveal the many forces at work in determining an object's value. The other myth is that "the archive resists change, corruptibility, and political manipulation" (2003, 19). The puppets and other objects used in performance are not simply passed down; rather, their use and value functions within, on, and in response to larger social networks. Raymond Williams describes art objects or texts for music and performance as "notations," which emphasizes their relationship to performance over their status as fixed material objects. The idea of notations suggests that "the relationship between the making of a work of art and its reception is always active, and subject to conventions, which in themselves are forms of (changing) social organization and relationship" (2005, 47). Studying the relationship between archive and practice in wayang kulit creates pathways to understanding how that relationship functions within social structures, especially gender relations. The puppets as notations work in several different ways—they are commodities with a certain kind of value, they are performers with the dalang, ritually powerful objects in their own right, and prized objects that can be sold to other dalang or tourists.

Valuing Puppets

At the art market in Sukowati, numerous puppets hang from a stand, creating a brilliant mosaic of colors swaying in the breeze. The woman watching the booth promises she will give me a "good price." An upmarket "antique" store in Ubud has several puppets sitting in wood stands, their colors are faded and the leather is worn thin. The shopkeeper assures me they are "very old" and "very valuable." Pak Tunjung tells me that once some tourists came up to him after a performance and asked if he would sell them some of the puppets from his box. He told them his puppets were "not for sale"; they were powerful ritual objects. The value of each puppet is determined by its quality, its context, and its use—sometimes the most valuable puppets are not for sale.

Each puppet is a work of art with delicate designs carved into toughened leather that is then painted many brilliant colors. Williams notes that the conditions of art making have often been overlooked (2005, 46), and examining the labor of designing and making puppets reveals how they are understood as tradition and act upon and within society. Pak Tunjung often carved his own puppets, but most dalang buy them from a *tukang wayang,* someone who specializes in making puppets. In addition to working with Pak Tunjung, I also studied puppet making with I Wayan Artawa, who learned how to carve from his father and every afternoon had several neighborhood children, mostly boys, over to learn how to carve. Pak Artawa explained that it was important to him that there would be others after him to carry on the tradition of puppet making, and that children were learning a profitable trade. Puppets are given value as commodities through labor and practice together with how the iconography of the puppets reiterates systems of hegemony in Balinese culture. I use the term *value* both to indicate a puppet's monetary value as a commodity and to indicate that the puppet represents and reaffirms the moral and spiritual values of the community.

Puppet carvers take their designs from existing puppets; Pak Artawa often traced his characters from the other puppets in his collection. He would place a piece of leather over the pattern, hold them both up to the sunlight, and use a felt-tip marker to trace the shape onto the leather (fig. 3.3). Many of the details were left out initially, though they were added once he carved the puppet. One day I was working on carving *ukil,* a design motif common in many puppets; it resembles a teardrop filled with little half moons. I carved the outside first and then worked on filling the inside. Pak Artawa explained that it was acceptable if I did not follow the lines of the design; instead it was important that all details of the carvings work together in balance and harmony.

Hobart remarks, "A puppet craftsman should be seen not as an innovator, but as the guardian of a cultural tradition in which his role is subordinated to that of socially dictated ideals" (1987, 69). On one hand, she is correct that tukang wayang work within the established aesthetics set by the audience and dalang who desire their puppets to conform to a certain standard or normative expectation. But this does not mean that there is only one way to carve a particular puppet. I've seen many variations of size, color, and ornamentation for the same character. Presently, puppet carvers will often borrow other people's puppets and make photocopies of them for patterns, and then other puppet makers borrow designs and ideas from those photocopies. This new method allows ideas to be easily shared from one artist to another, but perhaps the accuracy of electronic reproduction will eventually lead to designs becoming more static than they might have been if puppet makers continued to rely on memory to copy designs.

Figure 3.3. Pak Artawa shows two unpainted puppets. *Photo by author.*

When the Balinese artists I worked with spoke of a noticeable change from the typical forms or patterns, they would call these changes *inovasi,* or innovations. This term demonstrates that the artists are recognizing variation as a break from the tradition, and yet they approve of these alterations as in keeping with the intentions of the tradition. If a tukang wayang can negotiate the balance between inovasi and tradition well, it provides him with additional notoriety and power. Some dalang are known for and have benefited from their drastic innovations to the designs of their puppets. I

Wayan Wija introduced new puppets, such as a dinosaur and other highly articulated animal puppets, into traditional wayang. He made famous new puppet forms such as *wayang tantri*,[3] which focuses on Balinese versions of the animal fables known in India as the Tantri Kamandaka. These puppets have additional rods, strings, and sometimes even motorized parts to aid their movements. Pak Wija's designs and style of puppetry are being copied, so he is no longer the only one performing wayang tantri. Pak Tunjung, who studied with Pak Wija, was invited several times to perform wayang tantri while I was in Bali. He had to borrow animal puppets while he worked to make his own. Before one wayang tantri performance, Pak Tunjung complained that he was not as good as Pak Wija at performing wayang tantri, but the next day he boasted that the sponsors had praised his performance as being "better than Wija." I believe these comments demonstrate that Pak Tunjung recognizes the importance of the tradition as established by Pak Wija and that he was able to adapt the normative expectations of this new tradition and execute the performance with skill.

Young dalang, such as the students at the arts university, also experiment with puppet designs. One day when I visited ISI, I met a student in the *pedalangan* program (the wayang kulit department). He was focusing his studies on how to make the puppets and was well known for his beautiful and innovative designs. In fact, he received orders from many of the other students who desired his puppets. He showed me pictures of some of his puppets (on his digital camera), and at first glance these puppets looked Balinese, but closer inspection revealed that he was greatly influenced by Javanese puppet design. The student included some of the elongated features and carving motifs that distinguish the Javanese wayang puppets from the Balinese ones. He said that the puppets he designed were bigger as well and that the dalang students at the campus liked his puppets because they included the best from both styles.[4]

The colors of the puppets create another layer of meaning, even though often the audience can see only the black-and-white shadows. Pak Tunjung explained that the puppets perform for the gods and therefore must be decorated. I also found when performing with the puppets that the bright colors helped bring the puppets to life for the dalang and made them easier to characterize. Painting the puppets is another layer of specialized knowledge, and puppet carvers rarely paint their own puppets. In the past, paints were made from natural materials and each color required many layers; it was a time-consuming process (Hobart 1987, 79). The painters I observed now all use acrylic paints purchased from the store because these paints not only allow the painter to complete the puppets in less time but also allow for more brilliant and longer-lasting colors. Whether the paint is made from natural ingredients or purchased at a store, as a puppet ages and is exposed to the flame in performance, it loses its color and often turns a dark brown. Many tourist shops will take puppets of lesser quality and "age" them so they can be sold as antiques.

The quality of the puppet is an important consideration for a dalang, because it affects how the puppet moves, how easily it is manipulated, how long it will last, and the level of detail in the carving affects the quality of the shadow on the screen. I initially met Pak Artawa at Museum Puri Lukisan, where I took a class to learn more about carving and painting a puppet. When I arrived he was sitting at a table in the garden with several puppets in a stand for display. Pak Artawa began by showing me the difference between the puppets. Even though they were of the same character, Bima, they were of vastly different quality. One was very small and the details were few and large, while the other puppet was much larger and had many more fine details carved into the body. Pak Artawa explained that the finer details cast a much better shadow on the puppet screen and would make the puppet appear alive (*hidup*).

Pak Artawa then showed me a few samples of leather. Balinese wayang kulit are carved out of cowhide, and he explained that it was important to know how to pick the right leather for carving a puppet. The smaller Bima was made out of leather that was too thin; it would not hold a large design or fine details. Pak Artawa said the best leather was yellowish with the same thickness throughout and that it needed to be stiff but with some give.

Another time, I was at Pak Tunjung's when a leather seller visited with several samples. Each piece of leather was approximately four feet by five. Pak Tunjung looked at every one carefully before choosing. If he did not find any of the pieces to be of sufficient quality, he would not buy any leather but would wait for the seller to come again. Both Pak Tunjung and Pak Artawa emphasized to me the importance of being able to identify quality materials in order to make quality puppets. Puppets of lesser quality contain less power in both economic and social spheres. Obviously they cost less money, but to perform or own puppets of lesser quality transfers a lack of power or doubt of authority to the owner. Tourists can be duped, and are laughed at for their naïveté, but a Balinese dalang must know better.

Seeing the Puppets

Exhibits at the museum or puppets on display at a store or market are very different from the puppets in performance—because the puppets can be seen. Even though during a wayang lemah, or daytime performance, the puppets are visible because there is no screen, the puppets are not "seen" because the audience is not watching. The material object of the puppet is therefore not the primary source of power for wayang kulit. Examining the idea of "seeing," audience, and the puppets provides insight into how the puppets operate within gendered systems of power.

As a "seen" object, the puppet offers a unique relationship between performer and audience. Unlike theater or dance, where the performer is watched by the spectator, in puppetry both the performer and spectator watch the object. Puppet scholar John Bell (1997, 5) illustrates this function through the performer's and spectator's relationship to the object:

Performer ->->->-> object <-<-<-<-<- spectator

It is through this layered relationship, Bell argues, that puppets present a conduit for humans to come to terms with the material world; puppetry allows "a momentary alliance or bargain between humans and stuff of, or literally stuff *in* performance" (4). Bell theorizes puppets as objects that let us come to terms with death by allowing us to control the material, or "dead," world. Both the performer and the spectator are focused on the center, which creates a tension between the puppet as an object and the puppet as a living thing; it is at once both and neither. Bell adds, "With the movement possibilities of her body, and the vocal possibilities of her voice, the performer interprets, frames, and contextualizes the image in front of the spectators, and helps the communal experience of watching performance become one in which our own responses to the chosen objects are provoked" (5). Thus a puppet can be understood as an uncanny material object that signifies life through its design, movement, and cultural significance. I use Freud's term *uncanny* not because I want to attempt a psychoanalytic reading of the puppet in performance. Instead, I use the term as it refers to something that can be both foreign and familiar at the same time; it suggests life in the inanimate and endows the object with status as something strange.[5]

Wayang kulit further complicates the relationship Bell describes because not only is there the puppet in performance, but also there is the shadow. The ability to see is connected to ideas of power in Bali. Margaret J. Wiener explains: "From a Balinese perspective, power is enmeshed not merely in the visible world of social relations but also in the invisible world of 'spiritual' relations. It is in fact the latter that makes the authority of a person in the former possible at all" (1995, 10). The relationship between the dalang, puppet, shadow, and audience demonstrates Warner's point. The dalang can see the puppet, but the audience, like the people in Plato's cave, cannot—they can see only the shapes and not the real thing. The shadows of the puppets on the screen are not clear representations, because the angle and the flickering of the light source distorts and blurs the puppet form. The dalang, from his position behind the screen, performs his relationship to the community—he has the position of seeing, which is a position of power.

Women are removed from this system of seeing because they are rarely given the opportunity to watch the performance. Even if they are nearby, the women do not have the leisure to sit and watch; rather, women are busy preparing food, distributing offerings, or minding children.

In addition to the visible performers—the dalang and puppets—the act of performing wayang kulit invokes invisible spirits to provide assistance. When a dalang chews betel nut before the performance he is calling on the *kanda empat*, or four mystical siblings, to guide and protect the performance (Hobart 1987, 133). In Bali the kanda empat are believed to manifest at birth in the form of amniotic fluid, blood, placenta, and the vernix caseosa. These spirits are then believed to accompany each person throughout their lives. Even after death, the kanda empat remain in spirit. If the kanda empat are treated well, honored with offerings and remembered in thoughts and prayers, they will assist and help that person. However, if they are forgotten or misused, the kanda empat will cause trouble or harm.[6] The kanda empat are also cosmically connected to the four directions, representing four deities or aspects of humanity. The kanda empat connect the visible, or sekala, to the spiritual realm, or niskala, and to the gods.

The kanda empat are called upon to assist the performance in both the visible and the invisible realms—for example, when the dalang opens the puppet chest he recites a mantra that invokes the Four Dalang to guard him. The Four Dalang are connected to the visible body of the dalang through the performer's heart and voice; they provide protection and assist in creating a successful performance. The potential spiritual association of the Four Dalang reverberate into the niskala because the they are sometimes said to represent the four colors—white, black, yellow, red—that are associated with the guardians of the four cardinal directions or the four primary deities (Iswara, Brahma, Mahadewa, Wisnu). These Four Dalang are also thought to be the first dalang (Hooykaas 1973, 17). Zurbuchen explains the complex relationships linking these visible and invisible presences:

The Four Dalangs are logical counterparts of the Balinese Kanda Empat, four birth-siblings who accompany each human soul from conception through life and on after death. It seems as though the Four Dalangs are a special form of the protective and strengthening Kanda Empat, who are also, in turn, the microcosmic version of the macrocosmic four directional guardians. (1987, 131)

During the performance, the Four Dalang are replicated and given physical form within the bodies of the four servant characters, Twalen, Merdah, Delem, and Sangut.

As the kanda empat are linked to the body of the dalang in ways that reverberate through the performance and the physical and spiritual worlds, a woman's body disrupts the universal bodies represented by the Four Dalang within the performance because the Four Dalang are assumed to be male. Women playing gamelan or dancing *kecak* (monkey chant dance), also traditionally male spheres of performance, do not carry a similar spiritual significance such as embodied within the four invisible dalang. In performance, women dalang trouble the power of seeing as a means to connect the visible and invisible worlds in many ways.

Seeing Gender through the Puppets

Hobart makes a distinction between what she sees as the fixed iconography—the puppets, voices, and movement—compared to the fluid stories and notes that both work together to "articulate values, norms, rules, and ideals which relate to the social life of the people as well as to certain features of the social structure" (1987, 173). The iconography of the puppet is not "fixed" but adjusts to a society that is constantly changing. Even so, there are features of a puppet that can be read like a language or a text. This does not imply that the iconography is static but rather that through convention those details can be "read" for meaning. Because the puppets work together with the performer, it is necessary to understand the puppets as a visual signifier within Balinese society.

It has become cliché, and not wholly accurate, to say that the stage is a type of mirror reflecting society. It must be recognized that the power of the images onstage lies not in their reflexive quality but in how a performance enters into the discourse of reality. The puppets convey meaning to the audience through their iconography as well as their use. The size, shape, and decoration of the puppets function like a language, in that meaning is established by "collective behavior—or what amounts to the same thing—on convention" (Saussure 2001, 965). These conventions are established through repetition and therefore develop currency as objects and practices of "tradition." Judith Butler calls meaning established through repetition "reiteration." I have chosen Butler's term because it clarifies meaning as an ongoing process—likewise, matter is not static, but also constructed. Of matter, Butler writes, "The classical configuration of matter as a site of *generation* or *origination* becomes especially significant when the account of what an object is and means requires recourse to its originating principle" (1993, 31). She argues that matter is not only something produced, but rather fluctuates within a context of history and culture. Matter is constructed; Butler explains that "construction is neither a subject nor its act, but a process of reiteration by which both 'subjects' and 'acts' come to appear at all. There is no power that acts, but only a reiterated acting that is power in its persistence and instability" (9). Wayang kulit is based in highly codified and repetitious systems of convention, where ideals are displayed and reinforced within a public domain, requiring the performers to conform to the audience's expectations, thereby creating a performance that thus reiterates and reinforces those expectations. The physical object, or puppet, works as a system of representation in wayang kulit, and discourses of gender are expressed through those puppets.

Museums in Bali and around Indonesia often include wayang puppets as examples of art and cultural identity. These exhibits rarely feature any puppets of female characters—even when the display is meant to represent a "complete" set of puppets. Setia Darma House of Masks and Puppets in the village of Mas provides some of the best examples of wayang in Bali, and includes exhibits of several genres of wayang puppets. The vision of the museum is "to inspire people to learn about the culture of the past for the benefits of the present and future life" (http://www.setiadarma .org). The puppet sets were commissioned for the museum by well-known puppet makers in Bali and are displayed along a *gedong,* or banana log, as if they were waiting to be used in performance. The kayonan is in the center and the puppets are displayed from alus to kasar, extending to the right and left of the kayonan. Each appears to be a complete set—or to feature the puppets that are most important to that genre of wayang. These exhibits offer insight into how female puppets are displayed to reflect ideologies of gender and sexuality in Indonesia.

Gender ideology, or that which "spells out expectations of how men and women should behave according to their ascribed sex," in Indonesia has changed over time (Blackburn 2004, 8). Each region has certain customs, or adat, according to gender—for example, the matrilineal Minangkabau of western Sumatra have very different ideologies of gender than Bali. Over time, as the nation coalesced, national gender ideologies replaced or exist with those based on adat. The Dutch, through education, brought Western gender ideologies and in the twentieth century—notions of gender equality as well. The Japanese occupation (1942–45) emphasized women's roles as helpers to men, as wives, mothers, workers, and sometimes prostitutes. Independence required women to serve their country by serving their husbands, but some women also took leadership roles, and educational and career opportunities expanded as well. The New Order period (1965–98) especially had strong, and rather restrictive, notions of gender roles that it promoted nationally:

> Women should play their part in ensuring social stability, implementing development plans and reducing the birth-rate. In the early years of the regime women were seen solely as housewives and mothers. The term, *kodrat,* meaning

inherent nature, was frequently on the lips of government spokesmen in relation to women: their *kodrat* destined them to be carers and educators of the younger generation. (Blackburn 2004, 25)

The New Order emphasized that women were *ibu,* or mothers, and men were *bapak,* or fathers. Men had access to power outside the home while women were in charge of the home. Images of the ibu and bapak dominated social and political discourses. Since the fall of Suharto, many of these ideals remain dominant and influential. Susan Blackburn (2004, 9–11) is careful to note that there are often gaps between hegemonic ideologies related to gender and actual everyday practice. Additionally, throughout the twentieth century there were and still are many women's organizations working for and with women around Indonesia. The puppets of female characters must be understood within this complex web of discourses.

The connection between puppets in a museum and puppets in performance may seem tenuous. Each exists for a different purpose, and a somewhat different audience, but as Hildred Geertz argues, there is a deep connection between visual images and society in Bali. "Only through careful explication of the major references and allusions of these images can we outsiders begin to understand the worlds that they invoke and, at the same time, create" (1994, 3). The exhibits of the puppets, especially as they display gender, provide another venue for understanding the relationship between tradition and social hegemony as expressed in the arts.

As explained in chapter 2, the main system of visual representation lies along the scale of two primary types: alus and kasar. *Alus* roughly translates as "refined," and *kasar* is "unrefined." Each character often has traits that are both a little alus and kasar, reflecting the dual nature of people. "Good" characters, often called characters of the right, such as the Pandawas, are often the most alus. In contrast, the "bad" characters, or characters of the left—such as the raksasa, or ogres, and the Korawas—are often the most kasar. Right and left refer to the dalang's right or left—the audience would see these in reverse in performance. In the museum the viewer sees the puppets from the perspective of the dalang. Alus and kasar do not equal good and bad in Bali, and those categories are not absolute. For example, Arjuna (fig. 3.4, right) has very delicate features and is clearly alus. In contrast, his brother Bima (center) has bulging eyes and a large frame. Bima is far more kasar than Arjuna, but this speaks to his temperament, rather than being a judgment of good versus evil. The third puppet, Niwatakwaca (left), is the king of the raksasa and is clearly kasar.

For female characters, the range along the scale of alus and kasar is quite limited. In fact, many female characters, if observed side by side, show little variation. The shape of the eyes, the build, color, and height are all pretty much the same, and the primary distinction between female characters is the tilt of the head. Some are looking down and others are gazing straight ahead (none of

Figure 3.4. Alus and kasar characters: (*from left*) Niwatakwaca, Bima, and Arjuna. *Photo by author; puppets by I Wayan Tunjung.*

the females are gazing up). So they might be divided between alus and more alus. Examining the female forms allows the observer to read their "bodies" like a map that provides insight to how females are fashioned and integrated within the hierarchies of Balinese society. In order to understand the female character as portrayed in wayang kulit, one must remember that the key differentiation is between alus and kasar.[7]

This raises the question, are female characters more alus than the male ones? The answer is not simple, and Marc Benamou notes three possible answers to this question: "1) men are more alus than women, 2) women are more alus than men, 3) men are both more alus and more kasar than women" (2002, 176). The issue becomes complicated because to be alus is not only a physical attribute but also a sign of spiritual power that is therefore accessible only by males. Women are of lower social status, the argument continues, because they are not allowed the same spiritual power or authority as men, so therefore they could never be as alus, and men are more alus than women because they are allowed higher status in society and in religion. For females, alus is reduced to primarily a physical or outer trait; it is a sign of meekness rather than a sign of agency and power. Women, as expressed through alusness, are valued for their kodrat: their meekness, shyness, and obedience to their husbands and fathers.

For his research, Benamou (2002, 278) asked several Javanese musicians and dancers to rate a list of wayang kulit characters as most alus and most kasar. The responses he received varied considerably; some ranked a female character as most alus and some a male. However, several respondents expressed dissatisfaction at having to rank male and female characters together on the same scale; for them it was not possible to compare males and females. This reluctance further demonstrates how *alus* has a different meaning as applied to women than it does for men.

The appearance and role of women in Balinese society has changed over time; likewise the appearance and use of female puppet characters has changed. It is difficult to trace the history of iconography in wayang because puppets are rarely dated—and leather and paint quickly corrode in the tropical climate of Bali. Old puppets are highly valued for their spiritual power and monetary worth as antiques, so often puppets are "aged," or reported to be older than they might actually be. The female puppets reflect the current social situation and prescribe best behaviors for the audience, or viewers. Each exhibit draws from the aesthetics of alus and kasar, the tale the puppets tell, and the combined meaning of appearance and story.

The exhibit of *wayang parwa,* or the Mahabharata story, made by I Wayan Nartha in 2004 contains only two female puppets. One is Kunti, the mother of the Pandawa brothers. The other puppet figure could be one of several other important female characters—it is not clear which one. Most of these characters are wives of the Pandawa brothers. The exhibit demonstrates the minor role that female characters play in telling stories from the Mahabharata. Kunti is the most commonly used character and the other female characters are not distinct. Female puppets are often "used by the dhalang for female characters as needed—they are like a 'wildcard' for female characters" (Katz-Harris 2010, 97). The women characters are positioned as most alus because they stand closest to the kayonan. Kunti is a little larger than the other female puppet, but as mother of the Pandawas she is positioned to be more alus than the other female character. One of the women dalang, Ni Wayan Nondri, told me that Kunti, a powerful woman, was her favorite character "because [hers] is the story of the birth of the Pandawas. She has five babies. She treats them the same and she is very giving. I like her and I think she is someone I must imitate. If it was not for her we would not have the Pandawas, and then we would not have the Mahabharata. We must have her." Women in Indonesia are most valued as mothers and wives—these roles define women as alus and thus are given value within Balinese society. Kunti is the most alus, or possesses the most kodrat, because she best represents the ideal of a loyal wife and devout mother.

The display of *wayang Ramayana* puppets made by I Made Sidja (fig. 3.5, top row) offers a warning to women who might trespass the feminine ideal of loyal wife and mother—or betray their kodrat. Sinta (also often called Sita), the princess who was abducted from Rama by the demon Rawana, appears on the left side of the screen. Rama is on the right side. In the story, Rama finally rescues Sinta but requires her to undergo a trial by fire to prove her chastity and loyalty. She passes the test but remains shunned by Rama, who worries that his subjects will doubt her fidelity. The clown puppets are closest to the center of the screen, and Sinta and Rama are both positioned next closest to the kayonan puppet on the right and left sides. Splitting the puppets in the middle emphasizes Rama's doubt.

The arrangement of Rama in relation to Sinta emphasizes the power he has over her—and that men in Indonesia have over women. Rama presents the image of an ideal man—he is as devout as Arjuna but strong as Bima in battle. Sinta stands to the left

Figure 3.5. Wayang Ramayana on display at Setia Darma House. *Photo by author.*

of the kayonan and her eyes face left. Her direction is like all the other puppets on that side. Rama faces to the left, or away from the other puppets positioned on his side of the screen. His gaze points toward Sinta, positioning her as an object of desire, which reiterates the power he has over her. Laura Mulvey (1975) connects looking to pleasure and power in a way that is explicitly sexual— looking functions as an act of power. For Rama, a man, looking is an action and demonstrates his power. Sinta "appears"; "women watch themselves being looked at" (Berger 1972, 47). John Berger further ascribes the act of looking with pleasure for the looker and moral condemnation toward the female image being looked at (51). Rama's doubts are reenacted through the mirrored gaze of the viewer upon Sinta.

Sinta "possesses the ideal feminine qualities, she is humble, gentle, and a faithful wife" (Katz-Harris 2010, 95)—but Sinta's figure also embodies the constant threat of perfidy that is contained within all women. The puppet of Sinta remains on the side of the screen with Rawana; her fidelity to Rama remains in doubt—a woman cannot be trusted. Wariness of women, especially powerful women, resonates with Indonesia's recent history. Gerwani, a woman's organization dedicated to "equal labor rights for women and equal responsibilities with men in the struggle for full national independence and socialism," actively resisted women's kodrat (Wieringa 1998, 146, 148). Gerwani was abolished during Suharto's reign and became emblematic of a larger scheme to re-insubordinate women within the parameters of kodrat; its members were accused of sexual impurity, dancing naked, and severing the penises of generals (153). Like Sinta, the members of Gerwani were transformed from helpmates in the revolution to perpetrators of possible, though unproven, sexual misconduct. A woman's kodrat remains intrinsically connected to her sexuality within the proper enactment of wife and mother. Under Rama's gaze, the figure of Sinta, because of her abduction (and the survival of that abduction), inhabits a space of suspicion. Rama, through looking, holds power over Sinta, and this power is explicitly sexual. A ruler's power and ability to care for his people is directly connected to his sexual power and fertility (Anderson 1990, 32). Rama's sexual power and Sinta's sexual misconduct are reinforced through the arrangement of the characters on the screen—invoking archetypes of behavior for the viewer.

The final exhibit with female puppets is the exhibit of *wayang Calon Arang* (fig. 3.6). This rare type of exorcistic wayang performance tells the story of a widow named Rangda Ing Girah, more commonly known as Calon Arang, who is versed in black magic. Calon Arang has a beautiful daughter named Ratna Manggali, but no one wishes to marry her because they fear her mother. Enraged, Calon Arang sends a pestilence to the town along with other disasters. The performance of Calon Arang in most villages lasts the entire night, features some comedy and many frightening witch and demon characters, and ends with a danced battle between the characters of Rangda and Barong. This battle rarely produces a winner; rather, cosmic balance is restored through the act of performance. The masks of Rangda and Barong are used in many different ceremonies and are often given offerings even when not

Figure 3.6. Wayang Calon Arong on display at Setia Darma House. *Photo by author.*

being used in performance. They are central figures in Balinese religion and society and symbolize Balinese unity and community (Stephen 2001, 145).

Wayang Calon Arang is rarely performed because it is considered dangerous. Pak Tunjung told me about a dalang friend of his; they went to school together and were close like brothers. He said this friend once performed wayang Calon Arang. Pak Tunjung warned his friend not to do the performance because it was dangerous, but his friend performed the Calon Arang anyway. After the performance his friend became very sick; his skin turned black and he had to spend several weeks in the hospital. Pak Tunjung said his friend's illness was caused by the black magic in the wayang, and after that experience his friend no longer performed Calon Arang. Pak Tunjung commented that occasionally someone would ask him to perform Calon Arang; he would refuse and instead would offer to do any other kind of wayang story.

Unlike the other puppet collections on display, the set depicting wayang Calon Arang has many female puppets. There is one alus female, on the right of the screen, and it is not certain which character this puppet represents. (It is rare for a dalang to have a distinct puppet for each female character—the puppets are usually considered interchangeable.) This puppet could represent Ratna Manggali—Rangda's beautiful daughter. But in many versions of the story Rangda has female pupils (sisya), young girls from the village who have fallen under her spell. The sisya often perform a beautiful dance, but they also are said to feast on the corpses of the dead. The girls appear alus, but under that exterior lies danger and destruction. Placing this puppet on the right side of the kayonan, the "good" side, complicates both these possibilities. It suggests that Ratna Manggali does not follow in the dangerous footsteps of her mother—that despite her dark origin, she is pure in heart. If the puppet represents one of the sisya of Rangda, the placement indicates that their true origin, as daughters from the village, usurps their new status as students of the dark arts. Both possibilities communicate that when it comes to women, looks can be deceiving.

Bad women can become good and good women can become bad; their status is fluid. The form and shape of a single character can fluctuate, especially when it comes to the personages associated with Rangda (Emigh 1996, 66). The many male characters lined up with her are all quite kasar, as if size and strength are required to keep this female under control.

On the left side of the screen there is a demon hiding from view. His figure is obscured by a brown puppet with pendulous breasts; this puppet is likely the true figure of Ratna Manggali. Her ugly kasar body points toward her dangerous and even more kasar mother. The use of dual personages to represent Ratna Manggali reinforces the belief that "the witch is essentially a hidden enemy, although an apparent relation or neighbor" (Hobart 2003, 119), because the disfigured Ratna Manggali might also be the beautiful character on the right of the screen. The pretty female might also dance for Rangda and eat the entrails of dead bodies. The large bodies of the women on the left obscure and dominate the few male puppet characters. These puppets serve as a warning of what happens when women do not prioritize their roles as wives and mothers under the control of husbands.

It is not unusual that there are two puppets on the left of the screen that represent Rangda. Having more than one representation of Rangda is typical in Bali. Most of the temples have more than one Rangda on display at ceremonies. Rangda might be understood as a type with many different specific personages (Stephen 2001 141). The puppet figures capture the horrors of the witch Rangda, so wonderfully described by Clifford Geertz:

> Rangda, danced by a single male, is a hideous figure. Her eyes bulge from her forehead like swollen boils. Her teeth become tusks curving up over her cheeks and fangs protruding down over her chin. Her yellowed hair falls down around her in a matted tangle. Her breasts are dry and pendulous dugs edged with hair, between which hang, like so many sausages, strings of colored entrails. (1975, 114)

Rangda functions as the ultimate manifestation of magical power in Bali. The mask alone is thought to contain sacred, potentially dangerous energy. Like a dalang who might undertake performing wayang Calon Arang, the dancer who wears the mask of Rangda must contain "strong spiritual power" and "be a Wong Sakti or priest" (Bandem and deBoer 1995, 110). Even though Rangda represents the suspected dangers of uncontained female power, she also represents fluidity and uncertainty within gender and power in Bali. She is a character of evil transformation, a *pemurtian* (a supernatural being with many arms and heads), who "represents the awful face of divinity, without respect to gender or character" (111). The puppet Rangda, as an index for the many manifestations of Rangda in Bali, destabilizes power as associated with specific genders.

Calon Arang emphasizes the dangerous aspects that all women are thought to potentially contain. In performance the dalang calls the witches from the area to attend (Hobart 2003, 114). I attended one such performance at the Pura Delam, or temple of the dead, in southern Ubud. I was the only woman watching the performance in the eerie setting of the graveyard in Monkey Forest. The other men there indicated displeasure at my attendance and were very surprised when I responded to their questions in Balinese and Indonesian—perhaps they thought with my blond hair and blue eyes that I was a local witch. Taken together, the different female puppets in the display of wayang Calon Arang provide many different narratives of femaleness as alus and kasar, good and dangerous. They explain how Balinese women, even within national ideals of wives and mothers, negotiate complex identities in relation to tradition and modernity.

Unseen Power

The practice of wayang kulit connects tradition to hierarchical structures within Balinese society, but the practice of wayang kulit also assigns value to the puppet as an object. The Balinese believe that puppets should have long lives; a puppet that has been around for a long time is said to have a lot of spiritual power, or taksu.

The kind of taksu that can exist in a puppet was demonstrated at a performance for a family celebrating the final stages of a cremation ceremony. Pak Tunjung was given a very old puppet that had been in the family for generations (fig. 3.7). The puppet was kept in the family temple and given daily offerings. The family wanted it to be part of this ceremony because the person who had died was born on Tumpak Wayang; this is a dangerous day to be born because it is the day celebrating the birth of the puppets. People born on Tumpak Wayang must hold special ceremonies to ask the puppet gods, known as *sanghyang ringgit*,[8] for forgiveness or else they will be plagued with illness and misfortune in this life and the next.

The old puppet was carried out on a platter and was hidden under a white cloth by some of the older members of the family sponsoring the performance. When they got to the area behind the screen, Pak Tunjung took the puppet. He later told me that when he touched the puppet it was as if a jolt of electricity went through

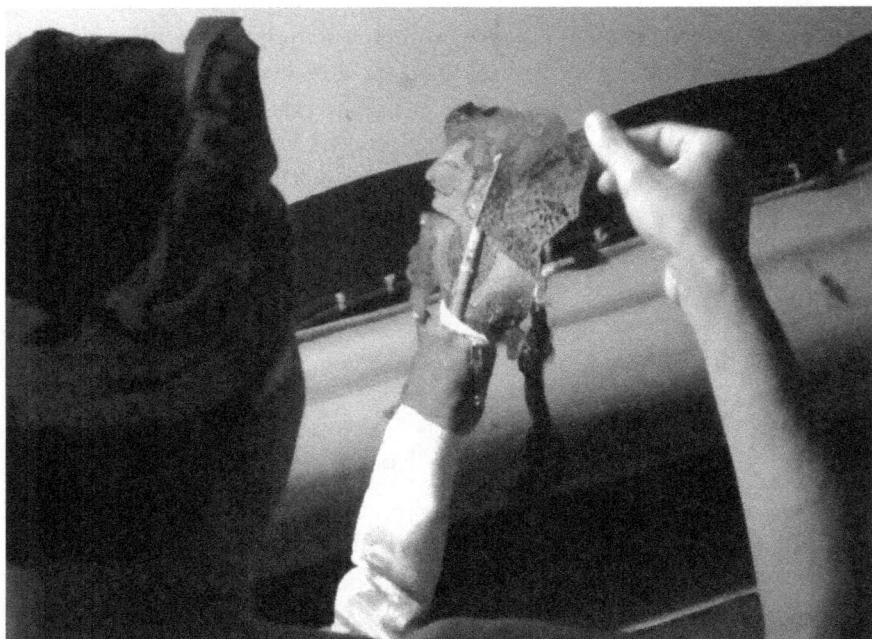

Figure 3.7. Pak Tunjung is given an old puppet. *Photo by author.*

his body. One of his assistants, sitting to his left, began to shake; he was made dizzy by the power contained in the puppet. Pak Tunjung wanted to respect the puppet, but he also wanted to be able to give a good performance. So after blessing the puppet and giving it offerings, he set it to the side for the show. It was never used—but it stood at the edge of the stage like an additional silent audience member. At the end of the performance it was placed next to the kayonan for the ceremony to make holy water (a major priestly function of the dalang is to make holy water). Finally, the ancient puppet was re-covered and carried back to its place in the temple.

Pak Tunjung explained that if a puppet contained enough taksu, it did not need to be used in a performance to have an effect. Often he would receive requests from people in the village to either sit near or meditate close to his puppets. Many of his puppets were very old and used in performance for a couple of generations; when he used them in performance it appeared as though some of them were in danger of falling apart.

A successful dalang must practice and work hard; each skill builds on the next. Pak Tunjung told me about an older student of his. Pak Tunjung sighed that the student did not want to learn one thing at a time, but instead wanted to learn everything at once, and that because of this the student was not very good at anything. Pak Tunjung said it is very important for all the elements of the performance to balance together, and that one of the hardest things for a dalang to do is to get the voice, the cepala, and the puppets to all work with the music. If these things do not work together, the performance is not good. Pak Tunjung explained that it requires patience in order to become a good dalang. The physical work prepares the way for the spiritual—the magic of wayang kulit happens in the body.

In order to clarify this point, Pak Tunjung showed me a two-page article in *Taksu,* the local Balinese monthly magazine on art, religion, and culture. It describes what a dalang prays for at the beginning of a performance: for his voice to be clear, his head to remember, and his body to be strong. These are the most important skills of a dalang; if he has them there is not much else he needs. Pak Tunjung said a performance could be given with just one other person to play music and that the most important puppets to own were the ones necessary to tell the stories from the Mahabharata. If a dalang has those puppets he does not need much else to tell any of the other stories.

Pak Tunjung said he really liked the magazine because it talks about how culture and religion are important and intermixed in Bali. He demonstrated with the puppets:

> TWALEN: OK, I would be happy to answer a question from someone in the audience. Who has a question? Yes, go ahead, where are you from?
>
> AUDIENCE MEMBER: I am from America. I was wondering if you can tell me about the difference between culture in Bali and culture in America?
>
> TWALEN: Yes, I can answer that. I think sometimes Americans feel like they do not have any culture— but that is not true! Americans have culture, but it is just different than culture in Bali. There are lots of different kinds of culture in America and each person can do different things. In Bali, culture is important because it is close to our religion. We have many different performances in Bali, like wayang, *topeng,* and *gambuh,* and these are important because they bring people closer to their spiritual side. Perhaps that is what is missing in America? They do not have something like that to make them more spiritual.

Through this scene, Pak Tunjung demonstrated the close ties that art, culture, and religion have in Balinese society and that the Balinese rarely consider one without the other two. As I learned more about wayang kulit, I learned more about the "magical" or spiritual aspect of this art form, and that these spiritual aspects are just as important as the performance techniques or good puppets.

Part Two

NISKALA:
THE INVISIBLE REALM

Chapter 4

RITUAL TRADITIONS
Becoming a Dalang

A Balinese dalang (puppeteer) told me: "Pray to
your god inside you before you pray to the gods in
the temples. If you cannot find it, try to find it while
you pray to the gods in the temples."
—I Wayan Lendra (1995, 153)

The dalang not only undergoes ritual as his or her connection
to the invisible world but also connects to that invisible world
through his performance. I write about the rituals associated with
wayang kulit and how the performance functions as ritual within
Balinese religion to elucidate the unseen as connected to systems of
hierarchy and power within Balinese society. There are many simi-
larities between tradition and ritual and how they function within
Balinese society, but it is important to remember that I am using
these terms as distinct, yet often intertwined, categorical frameworks even when describing the same phenomenon in relation to
my research. Tradition can refer to rituals in that rituals are often
traditional, but there is also a secular function of tradition that does
not transfer to ritual. Even so, much of the power wayang kulit
holds within Balinese society is an effect of its ritual properties and
its relationship to ritual.

There is a great deal of magic and mystery within the practice
of wayang kulit as it connects to ritual. Catherine Bell prefers
using the term "ritualization," instead of ritual, in order to "draw

attention to the way which certain social actions strategically distinguish themselves in relation to other actions." Ritual privileges some activities over others, creating a distance between the "sacred" and the "profane" (1992, 74). For the Balinese, any activity that mediates between the sekala and niskala realms should be understood as "ritualization" in that these activities are set apart and given special status within Balinese society. Within these activities, there are hierarchies based on who is involved, where the activity is performed, and when it is performed, and these things together effect the desired or actualized outcome.

I use two different styles of writing in this chapter: first one that emphasizes my own experience in the field and then another for the analysis of that experience. I do this in order to problematize the relationship of identity and spirituality in Bali in regard to tradition, ritual, and power as I, a foreigner and a woman, work to occupy this complex position in Balinese society. Ritual operates as a system of knowledge in Bali that requires the involvement of many different people doing many different things. Each person, even each dalang, will have a unique experience—"the key lies in acknowledging variation as a distinguishing characteristic of [Balinese] society" (Barth 1993, 14). I am not attempting to provide an authoritative overview of the individual ceremonies; rather, I am writing from my own experiences in order to better understand the roles these kinds of rituals play within the framework of Balinese society.

Moving through the Unseen: Ritual Purification

A few days after receiving the invitation to perform, my friend Kadek and I were able to meet together with Pak Sedana at his home, in Denpasar. He said that the steering committee for the Ubud Festival had just left his home a couple of hours ago and that they were very excited that I was going to perform in the festival. Pak Sedana wanted to talk to me about some of the logistics of the performance. He asked how long I thought I could perform, would I want an LCD projector, how many musicians, and so on. I told him I thought the performance would be about an hour, that I preferred to use an oil lamp and not an LCD projector or electric light, and that four musicians, as typical for wayang parwa, would be enough. I also explained that I needed to confirm with Pak Tunjung, my teacher, before finalizing any of these decisions.

Pak Sedana said I needed to go through several rituals before giving the performance, and therefore I needed to consult with a priest to determine the proper procedures. Kadek promised to help and said that her cousin, I Made Sumantra (Guru Made) who was a balian, *or lay priest, would be able to provide leadership. Pak Sedana explained that there were rituals in order to become a dalang and that it was also very important for every dalang to make an offering before the performance in order to ask for the help of the gods, while after the performance, the dalang must make another offering thanking the gods for their presence and assistance. Pak Sedana noted that these were not prayers for a good performance; rather, they functioned to acknowledge the required energy and needed cooperation from the gods. As part of my preparation I would need to go to several holy springs, and the day of the week I was born would determine how many springs were required. Pak Sedana boasted that he had gone to thirty-seven holy springs when he became a dalang. Later, I consulted with Guru Made, who determined that because I was born on a Friday I would need to go to nine springs. Kadek smiled and added that nine was a very auspicious number because it is the number three, three times; she felt this was very lucky. Guru Made promised to organize the trip and Kadek added that her mother was an offering expert and she would consult with her about what offerings we would need.*

I learned that becoming a dalang demands more than just learning how to give a performance; ritual initiation connects the dalang to the community of persons, ancestors, and gods in Bali. James Peacock articulates a way to think about my ritual initiation in relation to the practice period where I learned the logistics of performance. He writes that the physical training for performance can be understood as a kind of mediating process that moves the performer from everyday life into the situation of the performance. In theater, rehearsals form this period as the actors learn their lines and blocking and incorporate these into the physical world of the play occupied by the scenery, lights, and costumes. In ritual, the correlative process is a rite of passage; Peacock explains the difference between the two: "Consonant with the argument that the sacred is more embedded in wider existence, rites of passage would be regarded as more a part of community life—spatially set apart to be sure, but obligatory, dictated by social norms shared by everyone in the community. Rehearsal, in contrast, is voluntary training pursued by specialists in performances" (1990, 209). My study of wayang kulit included rehearsal, but the rite of passage that I underwent over the period of a couple of months gave me recognition as a dalang and prepared me to give my first performances.

It is possible to study and perform Balinese arts without undergoing a ritual process as part of the training. Larry Reed, a skilled puppeteer and director who trained and often works with Balinese artists, has not, as far as I can tell, undergone a ritual initiation. Even so, he often invokes or uses ritual in his performances; for example, his production of *Sidha Karya,* which combines topeng, dance, and puppetry, begins and closes in ritual (Diamond 2001, 267). In his MA thesis, Pak Sedana writes about the importance of ritual initiation to accompany the practical training in performance (1993 11–13). By suggesting I undertake this ritual process, Pak Sedana was also able to connect himself to my work as a dalang and gain prestige as one of my teachers. It was Pak Sedana, not Pak Tunjung, who helped determine the ritual ceremonies that I would participate in before my performance: "the student will follow the traditions of both his teacher and his village during such rituals" (1993, 12). Ritual further enhanced my connection to Balinese arts and tradition.

Purification plays an important part not only in the process of becoming a dalang but also within the performance of wayang kulit. Water provides the primary vehicle for ritual purification within Balinese ceremonies because it brings about a state of spiritual, physical, and mental purity and power, or *suci* (Hobart 1987, 118). Before and after the performance the dalang together with the objects of performance are cleansed with holy water. Special performances of wayang kulit tell stories of purification and contain rituals to make holy water.[1] Holy water is "a sekala container of a niskala power" (Eiseman 1989, 51) and thus functions as a primary tool for connecting these two realms. By undergoing purification through visiting a number of holy springs, the would-be dalang links himself to both the physical geography of the island and the invisible or magical forces as well. On one day we went to three different locations.

After our early morning yoga class, my partner, Tina, and I dressed in our pakian adat, our traditional Balinese clothes. Today we were going to travel with Guru Made and his cousin, my friend Kadek, in order to go to several holy springs as part of my ritual initiation to become a dalang. After a special breakfast of yellow rice, vegetables, and tempeh we went down to the front of the compound.

The offerings that were needed for the ceremonies were being loaded into the car. Kadek explained that we were going to go to three different holy springs that day and therefore we needed three different sets of offerings. The back of the car was overflowing with flowers, fruit, and cakes, all placed in ornate arrangements within different baskets and trays.

The first holy spring was at Indra Kila Giri, about an hour's drive north of Ubud. I was excited to be going to the same place that Arjuna went to meditate in the story I was going to tell for my wayang kulit debut. The roads going to Indra Kila Giri were very steep. We drove through several small villages and enjoyed the beautiful views. As we got closer we turned off of the main road onto a small dirt road that kept getting narrower and narrower the further along our journey we went. At one point the car got stuck, but Guru Made managed to break free. As we traveled I studied the Kawi I needed to memorize for the performance, and gender wayang music played from a cassette tape.

We finally arrived at a large open field and stopped the car next to several other vehicles that were parked near the stairs that led to the entrance of the temple. There was a sign at the beginning of the path and in the distance you could hear the chanting of two priests over a loud speaker. Guru Made explained that there was an odalan, *or ceremony, going on at one of the temples on the mountain—the sound echoed all through the valley, filling the area with mystical noise.*

At the sign, there was a path leading down that soon became a series of very steep stairs. Kadek carried the large basket filled with offerings on the top of her head. Sometimes Guru Made would take the basket from her and help, but they would not let me have a turn. The views of the mountains were amazing, but we kept going without stopping to admire the view. Finally, we arrived at the bottom of the path; the holy springs were on the left and to the right was the pura, *or temple. The temple here was very small, but it was because the main temple for the area was further down, across a small bamboo bridge, and then back up the mountain. As we walked, several men carrying gamelan instruments passed us and continued on across the rickety bridge. I was relieved when Guru Made confirmed that we would not have to go all the way to the larger temple in order to complete the ceremony.*

Before going to the side with the holy springs we needed to set our offerings by the altar in the small pura. Then we walked over to the springs; there were two, one for men and one for women. We did not want to get our clothes wet, so we took off our pakian adat and tied an extra sarong around our bodies at chest level. Each spring had a wall built around the spigots where water was flowing out and splashing onto the ground. The path to the springs was slippery and the water was flowing slowly. I was surprised to see candy wrappers and other trash strewn about on the ground. The water in the deepest spots came only to my ankles. Kadek and I each stood in front of a spigot, and she instructed me to drink nine times and then splash the water onto my face and head before bending down so that I could be covered in the water. Because the water pressure was so low, Kadek and I assisted each other by splashing the water onto each other's backs. We repeated these motions at each of the three spigots within the enclosure before heading back out to change back into our clothes.

Then Guru Made, Kadek, and I returned to the small temple in order to give offerings and to pray. Tina was going to get a head start going up the stairs back to the car; because she was menstruating she was not able to bathe in the springs or go into the temple enclosures. Before she left, Kadek told her that if anyone asked, she should say she was selesai, *or finished, rather than admitting that she was menstruating. I thought perhaps it would make other people nervous if they learned that Tina was at the holy springs during her period.*

Once inside the temple, we kneeled before the altar in order to pray. Another family came into the pura at that time and kneeled beside us. The two small children with them kept staring at me as if it was not typical to see non-Balinese at this particular temple. Guru Made led the prayers and as we were finishing he gave us and the other family holy water in order to complete the ceremony.

After the ceremony, we collected the basket with the offerings and started walking up the stairs back to the car. As we walked we took turns eating snacks from the basket that had been part of the ceremony. Kadek explained that the gods take the essence of the offerings and that it is then auspicious for us to eat the remains. I was glad for the nourishment, and I think Kadek was glad that by eating we made the basket lighter for the ascent.

We did not see Tina until we reached the end of our climb, where she was sitting and looking very rested. She told us several people came by as she sat and waited and they invited her to come down and pray with them. Tina said that she told them "sudah," indicating that she had already been down to pray.

My experiences at the next two temples that day were similar to the first in that they each involved a journey, offerings, water, and prayers. When we got to the spring of the second, all we could see was a big industrial building. It looked like they had turned the spring into a wastewater treatment plant! Guru Made was really surprised—he said it had not been like that last time he went there. Kadek explained that the plant was to pump water to other places on the island, like Ubud. Even though there was a big plant there, we were still going to bathe in the spring. We had to climb over pipes and cross a narrow walkway to get to the spring. The actual spring area looked nice. The water was not very deep. I went up to the spring and Guru Made had me stand with my hands out, like you do when getting sprinkled with water after praying. He recited some mantras and put something green and brownish on the palms of my hands, my throat, and my forehead. I asked "apa itu?" (what is that?) and he responded "jangan pertanya— atau lari" (don't ask—or else run). I first thought his response meant the power of whatever it was would flee if I asked, but then I thought maybe he meant I wouldn't like the answer. I am thinking it might have been some kind of dung.

The final spring for the day was located inside a cave at the top of a steep hill. The water was very shallow, so we did not need to change out of our pakian adat but instead just waded into the dark water. We went into the cave and there was a dirty white cloth hanging from the ceiling that stretched from the entrance and disappeared into the dark. About ten feet in there were two spigots squirting water that we used for the ceremony. I was told not to drink from this spring but to just wash my hair and splash water onto my face while Guru Made chanted.

The ceremony described above is a kind of *mawinten,* or purification ceremony. My travels around the island and to each of these holy springs connected me to Balinese tradition through geography and action. I was personally affected by the experience, and with each holy spring we visited, I felt more ready to give my performance. The journey changed me. Edith Turner, wife of the late Victor Turner, writing with William Blodgett, Singleton Kahona, and Fideli Benwa, offers insight for examining ritual when one is both inside and outside the experience—and explains that experience is one way that rituals create meaning: "the ritual builds the symbols and not vice versa" (1992, 17). Through the ritual action my body was inserted into Balinese systems of symbology and order.

In order to understand how my body together with the actions of visiting the holy springs produced a certain kind of Balinese symbology marking me as a dalang, it is useful to apply Arnold van Gennep's classic theory of ritual initiation. Van Gennep defines a ritual initiation as "a passage from one situation to another or from one cosmic or social world to another" (1960, 10). He describes initiation as happening in three distinct steps or stages. The first are preliminal rites, or rites of separation; the second are liminal rites, or rites of transition; and the final step is postliminal rites, or rites of incorporation. Not all the steps are given equal time or weight within different instances (11). The actions of the ceremonies, together with the travel to and from each spring, suggest on both a small and a larger scale the structure articulated by Van Gennep.

Traveling to the location of a holy spring required a separation from my daily activities and spaces. We journeyed from a secular space, Ubud, to sacred spaces, the temples where the springs were located. Physical travel and physical space are common features of Balinese religious practices. The island itself is configured into sacred spaces depending on geography; the mountain in the center, kaja, is considered the most sacred and most pure, in contrast to the sea that surrounds the island, kelod, which is considered dangerous. Each are important, and many ceremonies will involve travel from one point to the other. For example, as part of a cremation the family will hold a ceremony and make offerings at both Besakih, the mother temple of Bali and the most kaja location, and at the sea. For me, the visit to each individual spring also included a period of separation as we traveled from the car to the spring itself. Often the journey took some time, and the steep steps were difficult to climb, especially in the restrictive sarong I was wearing.

Van Gennep states, "Sacredness as an attribute is not absolute; it is brought into play by the nature of the particular situations" (1960, 12). Driving in a car, climbing stairs up a hillside, or wearing certain clothes are not in themselves sacred. Our intention and circumstances determined whether the activity could be described as sacred and therefore be given special meaning within the Balinese context. Tina, because she was menstruating, could not participate in the sacred parts of the trip—and therefore driving around the island or climbing stairs contained a different meaning for her.

The washing in the water, giving offerings, and praying are the activities perhaps most easily identified as ritual, but within the context of the purification ritual they should be understood as

Van Gennep's second stage, the transition, or liminal, stage. Victor Turner describes the "liminal entities" of this middle stage as

> neither here nor there; they are betwixt and between the positions assigned and arrayed by law, custom, convention, and ceremonial. As such their ambiguous and indeterminate attributes are expressed by a rich variety of symbols in the many societies that ritualize social and cultural transitions. Thus, liminality is frequently likened to death, to being in the womb, to invisibility, to darkness, to bisexuality, to the wilderness, and to an eclipse of the sun or moon. (1969, 95)

During the ritual I was both a dalang and not-a-dalang; I was both pure and impure. Each visit, or ritual, at each holy spring contained this liminal phase. Turner argues that liminality reverses social structures in order to later reinforce them (1969, 125–27). I depended on the ritual knowledge of Guru Made to lead me through the prayers, mantras, and offerings properly. Outside the frame of this ritual, the dalang would have higher ritual and social status than a balian because he can make a type of holy water that a lay priest cannot, but for the purification ritual the would-be dalang must depend on another's ritual knowledge.[2] Stephen Lansing understands Balinese ritual as a "collective social project" to bring the world into an "idealized order" (2006, 124). Rituals reenact a complex system of interdependence, especially in the moments that might be marked as liminal, in order to reinforce socially based hierarchies and interdependencies. The balian and dalang have particular roles in Balinese society, but those roles are interdependent. The purification ritual activities serve as a demonstration of that social system.

The final stages are rites of incorporation, after which a person is welcomed back into society and his or her new status is acknowledged and recognized. In Bali "the basic aim of all the rites [of passage] is to purify and to provide the individual with the appropriate spiritual energy to exist peacefully, productively, and healthfully in a dangerous world." Additionally the rituals gave me a certain kind of spiritual power, or *kesaktian,* which allows the individual "to live correctly and successfully" (Eiseman 1989, 84). Van Gennep (1960, 13) notes, however, that a ritual of purification or passage will shift a person's social position from one realm to another, but only so far as that place is socially appropriate—and Eiseman's "live correctly and successfully" certainly supports that in the case of the Balinese. How can a woman become a dalang if that is not a socially appropriate role? Purification is such a common ritual in Bali that it alone could not make me a dalang. Another ritual would be necessary.

Transformation: Uniting the Seen and the Unseen

Hari Raya Sariswati is a special day to honor the goddess of knowledge and learning. Guru Made said that it would be an ideal day to hold a special ceremony in order to help me become a dalang and to "marry" (mesakapan) *me to my puppets. As the performance date got closer, I was plagued by nightmares and often didn't sleep at night because of barking dogs—dogs are more sensitive to invisible spirits and their barking means that there are more spirits around. Guru Made reassured me that the ceremony would give me confidence and a strong spirit. He explained that because of my training I was becoming much more sensitive to the niskala realm and that after the rituals and the performance I would be able to sleep because I would be protected.*

On the special day, I dressed in pakian adat and went over to Guru Made's house a little after lunch. Tina, my partner, was visiting and took part in the ceremony because Guru Made told me that Tina had a strong spirit and he wanted her there to be able to always protect me.

Guru Made lived just a little north of Ubud. It was a short trip on the motorbike, and when Tina and I arrived, Kadek was still unloading the offerings from the car and getting set up. She brought an orange in her purse and with it made us a tasty beverage called hot orange. I offered to help, but Guru Made assured us that the best thing we could do was to stay out of the way, so we drank our hot orange and watched him place the offerings and incense. Guru Made had a family temple up the stairs from his garden, and next to the temple was a room with another shrine where he worked with patients and performed healings. I had been to his house numerous times for both ceremonies and to visit, but I had never been this nervous. Guru Made placed offerings in the temple and at the shrine; as he set out the offerings he chanted mantras and lighted the incense.

Finally, Guru Made smiled and told us it was time for the ceremony to start, so we took off our shoes, walked into the temple area, and sat on the cushions next to Kadek. Guru Made and his wife sat together facing the offerings and they performed many steps of the ceremony together. Tina and I stood up so that Guru Made's wife could put water on our feet and palms. Next, she used different objects, like rice and an egg, to bless and "clean" away any bad energy from our bodies. At the end of the cleaning we had to move our arms in order to clear our auras, as Guru Made explained. The motion looked to me like we were trying to wave away smoke at the height of our waist. Then we sat back down.

The next step involved the five tastes. We were presented with a basket of five little green banana leaves, and in each leaf was a different thing that we needed to taste as part of the ceremony. They were bitter (coffee), salty (salt), sweet (sugar), savory (they would not tell me what that was), and sour (lemon). As we tasted each item, Kadek and Guru Made would giggle and try to make us guess what it was we tasted. It surprised me that they were joking because I felt that this was my Big Important Ritual, but for the Balinese, ritual is not that separate from everyday life. It is not a solemn occasion but a happy event shared with friends.

Later, Kadek explained that usually the ceremony would substitute spicy instead of one of the other tastes, but because my stomach cannot tolerate spicy food, they decided it would be better to replace spicy with something else. I asked if this would affect the efficacy of the ritual— shouldn't there be a "right" way to do it? Guru Made assured me that each ritual must be suited to the time, place, and circumstances of the moment. His explanation made me think that doing ritual in Bali was

Figure 4.1. Guru Made and his wife work together during the ceremony.
Photo by author.

more like making a stir-fry rather than baking a cake—you can change some ingredients and still have a good stir-fry, but you must follow a cake recipe exactly or it may well end up a disaster.

Following the tasting, I sat in front of Guru Made with my eyes closed, while he chanted mantras and touched my chakra points and the palms of my hands with water. I opened my eyes and mouth and he wrote a character on my tongue with his finger. While he did this I felt a surge of energy, like there was electricity flowing through my body. Then I moved to the side so he could repeat the same actions with Tina.

After we had both been blessed in this manner, we turned our attention to the two largest offerings sitting on the altar in front of us. The first offering was for confidence and physical strength. Guru Made said a mantra and we waved the energy from the offering toward our bodies. Next, the second offering was for the strength of spirit; again we waved the energy of the offering toward ourselves. Then we each ripped a leaf on the first offering, which symbolized that the offering had been used, and we each took a small bundle of flowers from the offering and tucked it into our shirts. Guru Made indicated that we should stand again so that he could anoint our heads with water from the ladle he used in the ceremony. Next, Guru Made and his wife each took some red, white, and black string (to represent Visnu, Siwa, and Brahma) and tied it around our wrists. After the ceremony we did not take these bracelets off, because they would eventually fall away. I had this memory of the ceremony tied around my wrist until December, and Tina had hers even longer.

Guru Made sent me outside the temple to get the puppets, so I retrieved Twalen, Merdah, and the kayonan. He then repeated each step of the ceremony with the puppets, anointing them with water, the egg, and rice; he gave them each the five tastes and chanted the same mantras. At the end he tied the same red, white, and black strings to the sticks of each of the puppets, and then the remaining puppets I had brought were blessed with water. Finally Guru Made handed me each of the puppets along with a bundle of flowers, which I placed in my puppet bag. This ritual symbolized that the puppets were "married" to me; they were no longer just objects, and I was spiritually tied to them *as their dalang. Guru Made explained that I needed to ask permission each time before using them and give them offerings regularly, even after I returned to the United States. After the ceremony, I felt a special connection with my puppets—I felt more like a dalang.*

Many scholars and Balinese assert that rituals are conducted to maintain balance and social harmony. The natural world exists in a constant state of disorder, and it is only through human spiritual and physical intervention that order can be attained (Lansing 2006, 123). This applies at both the macrocosmic level and to daily life and mundane concerns (Diamond 2012, 92). The concept of balance, or *rwa bhineda,* between order and disorder must be further complicated in order to understand how the mesakapan ritual made me a dalang—I need to rethink how balance might work within Balinese ritual. Catherine Bell notes that the ritual triad described by both Turner and Van Gennep relies on dualities in order for their theories to make sense, such as ritual/nonritual, leader/follower, before/after, and so on. She argues, through applying Derrida, that there is room for slippage between the social and ritual hierarchy, and this slippage might explain how I, or another woman, could insert myself into the ritual process to become a dalang without challenging the larger social system that defines a dalang. In regard to Bali, Diamond adds,

> While rwa bhineda permeates Balinese culture, even the perception of how "opposites" are defined is not absolute; changes in Balinese society challenge how binaries have been customarily applied. Thus while the performing arts themselves are also subject to social change, acts of performance are simultaneously employed to further the understanding of what constitutes harmony in the modern world as well as restore it. (2012, 92)

Rituals provide a tangible means through items and actions to connect bodies to social structures in dynamic ways. In order to understand how I could become a dalang though ritual, I will use the idea of transformation in relation to balance.

Transformation implies ongoing change, while balance indicates a move toward or a desire for stasis. Michele Stephen, following Hildred Geertz (2002, 62), argues that within Balinese cosmology all negative forces derive from positive origins, and thus "a constant flux or cycle of transformations of powers moving between positive and negative poles" presents a better way to conceptualize power in Bali. I am not so eager to abandon the importance of "balance"; rather, I am interested in the relation of balance to transformation. Ritual allows identities to shift and change; it is not about satisfying the needs of two opposing sides so they can exist in harmony. Instead, identities can transform in response to changes in the spiritual/social sphere in order to regain balance. Bell (1992, 105) describes Derrida's *différance* as a process of "free play" in which meaning is multiplied and destabilized as various signs and signifiers interact within the cultural field. Where dualism or balance suggests the possibility of stability within the system, Bell proposes a process where meaning is constantly created and never fixed.

In order to understand these slippages within the Balinese context, Stephen challenges the common notion that all of Balinese ritual and other religious activities focus on a return to balance between negative and positive cosmic forces as their primary aim: "in Balinese belief, all the destructive and negative forces present in the cosmos originate from creative, positive powers and, furthermore, possess the potential to return to their original positive state" (2002, 61). She proposes that transformation, rather than balance, provides a key framework for understanding Balinese practice. Although I would quibble with Stephen's dismissal of the usefulness of balance—indeed balance is evident in many genres of performance, architecture, and religious beliefs throughout Bali—I find that her interpretation of the role of transformation provides insight into how the ceremony of mesakapan works to make a dalang.

The different items and actions of the ritual provided a system of signs and signifiers that pointed to the idea of a dalang. Attempting to read the signs within the structures suggested by Bell's and Stephen's notion of transformation provides insight into how one can *become* a dalang. I am not attempting to provide an explanation for how the different items of the ritual might be understood by a Balinese priest; rather I am trying to understand how they fit within my interpretation of Balinese social systems and work as transformation. I join Lansing (2006, 1–6) in attempting to understand Balinese ritual in productive social ways both within and outside the Balinese worldview. Bell makes a differentiation between belief and ideology and some insightful observations about each:

> The traditional association of belief and ritual is also challenged by growing evidence that most symbolic action, even the basic symbols of a community's ritual life, can be very unclear to participants or interpreted by them in very dissimilar ways. . . . This suggests that some level or degree of social consensus does not depend upon shared information or beliefs, and ritual need not be seen as a simple medium of communicating such information or beliefs. (1992, 183)

Bell warns that each member of an audience or participant in a ritual might have a different idea regarding the meaning and significance in each object and, I would add, action of that ritual. Rituals do not levy control through shared belief, or to promote beliefs; rather, the power of ritual lies in its abilities to speak to a multiplicity of beliefs through consensus of form (186).

The ritual began with a defining of the space as "sacred" by Guru Made as he said mantras and placed the needed ritual offerings by the altar. Tina and I took off our shoes in order to enter the space, demonstrating our acknowledgment that this place was special. Even though Guru Made and his wife probably understood the significance of the space differently from Tina and me, we all experienced the space as ritual space, with the accompanying transformative powers. Henri Lefebvre sees space as something that is constantly being created even as it is being experienced. It is not a static truth, even though it might be experienced as such; rather, it is culturally, socially, and politically determined. "It is clear, therefore, that a spatial code is not simply a means of reading or interpreting space: rather it is a means of living in that space, of understanding it, and of producing it. As such it brings together verbal signs (words and sentences along with the meaning invested in them by a signifying process) and non-verbal signs (music, sounds, evocations, architectural constructions)" (1992, 47–48). Space functions as a kind of language or sign system, and as such, language, Foucault argues, is indicative of power.

The next step in the ritual served to connect our bodies to the sacred potential of the space, thus creating ritual bodies. Tina and I were blessed with rice, water, and eggs in order to "cleanse the bad energy from our bodies." Bell (1992, 96) describes how ritual often enacts a process to transform "nature," represented by the rice and other items, into "culture," represented by the idea of *dalang,* thus inscribing a "social body." It is this social body that contained the potential for me to enter the foreign system of Balinese dalangness because invisible forces and values are given a means to be realized ontologically. Likewise the tasting of five different foods connected our body to the Balinese social sphere; the foods were made by the Balinese and thus required effort to prepare and cook. One of the foods was swapped out for the usual spicy taste, indicating the flexible nature of ritual. Even for a woman and a non-Balinese, the ritual could be changed in order to accommodate difference.

The ritual reinforced the desired skills for a dalang, connecting intangible with tangible, in a couple of ways. First there were specific offerings to give me confidence and physical strength—my description of the practice of the dalang addresses why these would be important qualities. Guru Made also touched my tongue with holy water and drew a sacred character on its surface. A. L. Becker relates this action to the story of a Balinese king Aridharma; the king of snakes writes on the tongue of Aridharma in order to transmit knowledge. The action of writing on the tongue as a means to convey knowledge and wisdom exists throughout much of Southeast Asia and traces back to India—"the magic power of letters beyond the mere shaping of words is unsaid" (1989, 6).

Much of a dalang's power in society can be connected to his ability to speak and to his knowledge of sacred doctrines and texts. Anthropologist Carol Warren recounts the tale of a historically famous dalang, I Lisah, from the late nineteenth century, who was known for his masterful performances and spiritual power. In the story the dalang is called before the king to give a performance and the dalang refuses, even daring to address the king in low Balinese. Such disrespectful address was unheard of and the dalang was condemned to death. But I Lisah successfully challenged his sentence by demonstrating his knowledge of the *lontar,* or ancient palm leaf manuscripts, which state that a dalang may indeed address a king in this seemingly disrespectful way. The royal priest confirmed this assertion and the prestige of I Lisah was enhanced through the encounter. Warren concludes, "[the dalang's] power is grounded in two kinds of knowledge—one based on the written text and the other on his charismatic, publicly acknowledged access to the supernatural" (1998, 86). The symbol drawn on my tongue pointed to power based on charisma communicated through the voice and the power of the written word.

Finally each step of the ceremony was repeated with the puppets, specifically Twalen, Merdah, and the kayonan. The kayonan represents all things and therefore is able to stand in for all the other puppets in the box, both past and future. Adeline Hirschfeld-Medalia (1984, 219) learned from discussing this ceremony with dalang Pak Sumandhi that including the clown puppets represents the strong spiritual connection with the audience that the dalang must foster and possess in performance, which relates back to the dalang's spiritual connection to his own puppets. The bond established during this ceremony is so strong that many dalang refuse to perform with any other penasar than their own. Finally, this strong spiritual tie to the art contributes to the dalang's physical ability to execute the rigorous demands of a good performance.

Inserting a woman into the ritual to become a dalang subverts the ritual hierarchy (that through action a woman can assume a role typically reserved for men only—thus demonstrating the falseness of the construction that only men can be dalang), and yet the exception also proves the strength of ritual and thus serves to reinforce hierarchy. Through ritualization, a ritual body is formed. A ritual body "is a body invested with a 'sense' of ritual. The sense of ritual exists as an implicit variety of schemes whose deployment works to produce sociocultural situations that the ritual body can dominate in some way" (C. Bell 1992, 98). The sense of ritual, or process of ritualization, produces a body that is changed. In my case—my body was given *sakti*, or spiritual power, through my now physical and spiritual connection to the sacred objects of the puppets, thus enabling me to *be* a dalang. Ritual was the productive force that inserted me into the social structures of dalangness.

Negotiating the Unseen — Ritual Performance

My friend Kadek and I arrived in the village for the ceremony at around eleven in the morning. The streets were empty of cars and people, but a line of motorbikes, several rows deep, were parked outside a high wall that led to the bale banjar, *or community meeting place. A priest chanting scriptures could be heard over the loudspeaker, and gamelan music added to the din. Kadek and I glanced through those gates to see the many rows of offerings and photos to honor the dead that were displayed on elaborate tables and shelves. We did not go in but made our way through the entrance of a family compound next door; the compound was peaceful and quiet compared to the bustle of the ceremony. At the center of the compound sat Ni Wayan Suratni, alone, studying an open book, but as we entered she looked up to gesture that we should come over and sit beside her. Once we were settled she excused herself and returned a moment later with a tray containing small Balinese cakes and coffee. Ibu Suratni offered us the snacks and then went back to her studying. As we ate, several men, who would later serve as Ibu Suratni's musicians and assistants for the performance, came over to share the drinks and food with us. Off to the side an old grandma, wearing only a sarong, sat chopping food while watching two young children playing.*

Eventually, a man came over to tell Ibu Suratni that they were ready for her to come over to the performance place, and we followed her out. I looked forward to seeing her perform—it is a rare thing to see a woman perform wayang kulit.

The dalang is valued within his community because of the vital role he plays in a ritual ceremony. "[Ritual activities] mark him off from ordinary villagers and indicate something of the powers attributed to him" (Hobart 1987, 132). Many of the performance opportunities for women dalang were outside the ritual context because they were for competitions, government exhibitions, or in foreign countries. The ritual context, however, is where the dalang demonstrates his connections to unseen religious, and likewise societal, power. In this section I shall analyze two performances, given by two "outsider" dalang, or dalang that rupture the norm— myself and Ni Wayan Suratni. The context, reception, and frame of the performances demonstrate how wayang kulit functions as theater and ritual, reflecting and reinforcing cultural values and structures, while revealing the possible dangers that exist within this ritual performance.

The danger for Ibu Suratni hinged on how the performance functions as ritual. For Émile Durkheim the division between the profane and sacred is absolute: "In all the history of human thought there exists no other example of two categories of things so profoundly differentiated or so radically opposed to one another" (1961, 38). Durkheim argues that the two worlds never intermingle, a person or thing may pass from one to the other, but that even such a moment requires a kind of transformation that reinforces rather than challenges their incompatibility (39–43). In contrast, Richard Schechner asserts that ritual performance actively moves along a continuum and ritual is always becoming theater while theater is always becoming ritual. Building from E. T. Kirby's theory of the ritual origins of theater, Schechner suggests a useful continuum that illustrates the qualities of efficacy and entertainment in a graph. On one side is ritual, or efficacy, and on the opposite extreme is entertainment, or theater. Schechner lists the qualities of ritual as, "results, link to an absent Other, abolishes time—symbolic time, brings Other here, performer possessed—in trance, audience participates, audience believes, criticism is forbidden", and "collective creativity." The qualities of theater are, "fun, only for those here, emphasizes now, audience in the Other, performer knows what he's doing, audience watches, audience appreciates, criticism is encouraged", and "individual creativity" (1974, 467). Schechner's continuum, though perhaps a bit simplistic, provides a vocabulary for comparing my performance with Ibu Suratni's, and how each functioned within the scale of sacred and secular.

Schechner's framework is useful for analyzing a performance given as part of a cremation ceremony by Ni Wayan Suratni during May 2009. She performed wayang lemah, a specific type of ritual performance that is done during the day as a necessary part of a religious ceremony in Bali. The Balinese cremation ceremony is complex and has various steps, so I will give only a general overview here. After a person dies, he or she is buried in the ground at the graveyard at the Pura Delam, or temple of the dead. A corpse might remain in the ground for only a few months or up to several years, depending both on when a family has the financial resources and when it is an auspicious time for a cremation. Cremations can be for an individual and sponsored by a single family or cremations can be for multiple people and involve the entire village, so that participants can combine resources to mitigate the tremendous cost involved in these ceremonies. For the actual cremation a tower is built and paraded through the town to the cremation grounds. The higher caste—or the more important—the person was, the larger the tower. Recent royal cremations in the city of Ubud have had towers several stories tall. At the cremation grounds a series of purification ceremonies are held and finally the pyres are set on fire to grant the soul's passage to heaven, where he or she will await reincarnation. About twelve days after the burning, the members of the family will create elaborate effigies and offerings in order to have another ceremony where the effigies will also be burned and the ashes cast into the ocean. It is important that all the steps of the ceremony are properly executed to ensure the soul's journey into the next life, otherwise the soul will not be able to find its way and will remain on earth causing trouble for the family and members of the village. Wayang kulit is a vital ingredient in this complex ceremony.

It is not common for women dalang to perform for a ritual such as a cremation in contemporary Bali. In my analysis I want to examine how Suratni's identity as a "woman" dalang troubles some of the ritual characteristics of this performance. Schechner lists "results" as the first criterion, and that was certainly the purpose of this performance—to ensure that the soul of the deceased would find peace in the next life. But whether this was successful or not depends on the other elements. So I will come back to it later.

Three of Schechner's criteria—link to an absent Other, abolishes time/symbolic time, and brings Other here—must be considered together because a wayang kulit performance in Bali does all three. The performance both links to an absent Other and brings the Other here because the performance is primarily for the gods and spirits of the ancestors, who are called down to witness the rituals for the cremation and the performing arts like wayang kulit or topeng (masked dance). Performance is done for the gods' entertainment so that the ritual might be efficacious.

A wayang lemah performance happens during the day—so no screen is used. Instead, the dalang is visible to the audience; there is a string stretched across the front of the stage that gives the puppets support while the dalang performs. At the beginning of the performance the dalang knocks against the wood puppet box with a small hammer, the cepala, this indicates that the dalang is joining the world of the performance, already started by the musicians. Ibu Suratni knocked slowly and then gained speed, rhythmically playing her percussion in counterpoint to the music. With a nod to her assistant, Ibu Suratni reached her arm across her body and picked up the kayonan from her left side. The intricate design carved into leather of this puppet symbolizes the creation of the universe through the representation of the five universal elements: earth, fire, water, ether, and air. The kayonan always begins and ends each performance of wayang kulit, and can be used within the show as a prop or scenery, such as a mountain, vehicle, fire, thunder, or other entity as required. Ibu Suratni first held the kayonan puppet in front of her face while the musicians continued to play; this allows the dalang a quiet moment of concentration before embarking on the journey of the performance. She knocked the cepala again before the kayonan began to move and flutter with the opening movements of the performance; it floated and moved in the space right behind the string strung between the two banana logs; she occasionally tapped it, causing more vibrations. The choreography of this opening is set and executed by each dalang around Bali in pretty much the same way. The movements across the center of the playing area and from the different corners reenact the birth of the universe.

Through the movement of the kayonan the dalang links the past with the present so that both are joined and experienced simultaneously. The Balinese describe time as cyclic; people are reincarnated from one life into another, and performance is one place that enacts that kind of time. Also, the gods of the puppets are called down to be present within the performance. The dalang both speaks for them and makes them speak. This complicated relationship between dalang and spirits brings me to the next criterion, "performer possessed, in a trance." Although there is no sense that the dalang is actually possessed or in a trance for the performance, the dalang does experience an elevated status because he voices and controls the characters of gods through the puppets. Some dalang have explained to me that during the moment of performance they become unaware of their surroundings and focused only on the puppets and their actions. My teacher, Pak Tunjung, once complained of an upset stomach before a performance but then said during the performance he forgot all about it. Through the dalang the puppets come alive for the performance, and it is in that sense that the dalang is possessed.

Four of Schechner's criteria all relate to the position of the audience in relation to the performance, and many argue that these criteria indicate that there really should be no audience for a ritual. David E. R. George suggests that Pentheus was put to death by the

Maenads in Euripides' *The Bacchae* because he dared watch their ceremony; he was a "profanation of the ritual," because "communal, ecstatic, it was a magical mystery to be joined in, not observed" (1987, 128). Ritual does not or should not have an "audience"; rather, everyone is a participant. As Ibu Suratni began performing, however, more and more people gathered around the small area in order to watch the puppets. Women passed by carrying offerings from one part of the ceremonial space to another; they would often slow down to watch Ibu Suratni perform. I had seen many different dalang perform wayang lemah in many different circumstances but had never seen people watch the performance like they watched Ibu Suratni. At first I thought it might just be because the combination of a woman dalang, a video camera, and me—with my blond hair and traditional Balinese clothing—created quite a spectacle. The audience could be watching merely out of appreciation and curiosity. Balinese scholar and artist I Made Bandem suggested in a conversation with me that maybe women dalang have not continued as a trend because there is concern about whether a woman could manage all the different elements in a wayang kulit. He thought that maybe the audience watched Suratni's performance because there was a danger she might not execute the performance correctly, which would be disastrous for the success of the entire ritual.

At a certain part in the performance, the main priest indicated that the ceremony was coming to a close, and Ibu Suratni quickly ended the performance. All the members of the community sat to pray and then everyone headed home. The ritual was complete, for this day anyway.

In the end, Ibu Suratni's performance worked as ritual—but because she was a woman dalang there was the ever-present threat that it was *not* ritual. Durkheim leaves open a possibility for something that is not quite ritual and not quite theater and describes an in-between space that might be understood as magic. Thus, wayang kulit is closer to magic than it is to religion, because magic does not require universal belief or participation. Viewing wayang kulit as magic opens up the possibilities for it to work as ritual in a large number of different circumstances with many different people in the audience or performing as dalang. "The magician has no need of uniting himself to his fellows to practice his art" (Durkheim 1961, 58). Understanding the dalang as a kind of magician allows wayang kulit to function as both ritual and theater.

One day, near the end of my Fulbright fellowship in Indonesia, when I arrived at Pak Tunjung's house for practice I saw that the screen we had been using had been moved aside and an even bigger screen sat in its place. Well, the frame was there anyway—Pak Tunjung explained that he still needed to buy the fabric and get the screen made. He planned on giving the smaller screen to a friend to use in rehearsal. So for our lesson today we would work on the voice, and this gave us an opportunity to talk some more about a performance I had recently given for an odalan in the nearby village of Kutuh.

Pak Tunjung said that before a performance it was very important to pray and meditate because wayang kulit has very powerful magic and is therefore vulnerable to people who do "black magic." He warned that I needed to be careful. He then went on to explain that he was amazed because my performance that night was "full magic," especially remarkable because I was a woman dalang. He was impressed that a woman dalang could perform a complete story and that after seeing me perform, Ibu Arini and Pak Sedena, two professors from ISI who watched my performance, were also very pleased with it. On reflection, I was flattered by Pak Tunjung's praise, but I suspect he exaggerated my ability. I include this praise here not as evidence of my own skills in performing but rather to order to demonstrate how discourse translates into power for the dalang. The performance was "traditional" and therefore judged to be magically potent, which demonstrates a level of skill and power for the performer and her teacher.

Several events around my performance demonstrate how invisible power manifests in and around a wayang kulit performance. Pak Tunjung described how on the day before my performance he went to the temple in Kutuh to inspect the performance space; while he was there an old man with white hair and a long beard was watching him very closely. Pak Tunjung worried that this person had "bad magic," and Pak Tunjung had to plan what steps he was going to take in order to protect me. He said on the day of the performance he spent time in the temple meditating and praying for the gods to protect me and give me a good performance with "good power." When I arrived at Pak Tunjung's house before the performance, he blessed me with holy water and put a flower in my hair. Though I did not know it at the time, Pak Tunjung later explained that the flower would provide a shield around my body to guard me from "black magic." During my performance, Pak Tunjung said that he meditated some more and felt there was "bad magic" in the temple and that he had kept it away from me during my performance. Pak Tunjung concluded by saying again that my performance was very powerful and that he felt it was remarkable that I was able to do the entire story. After the performance several people requested oil from the oil lamp I used to light my screen. Audience members do this because they feel that the power of the dalang and the performance is absorbed into the oil during the performance and it will act as a healing salve. I was honored that they thought the oil from my performance might have these healing properties.

There is an element of danger to the invisible power associated with a wayang kulit performance. Pak Tunjung explained he once had another friend, a Balinese male, who had been studying wayang kulit with him. This person was asked to give a performance in his village, but he did not tell Pak Tunjung about the invitation. Before the performance he did not pray or give offerings in his family temple, and therefore he was able to perform for only fifteen minutes before he felt a sharp pain in the middle of his body. This friend had to stop the performance because he was no longer able to lift his arm nor move the puppets. The next day, by the time he visited Pak Tunjung, he could barely walk. Not only that, both arms were white, cold to the touch, and unable to move. Pak Tunjung said it was like the arms were dead. The man sat and waited while Pak Tunjung went into his temple to pray to the puppet gods and to make holy water; he then sprinkled the man with the holy water and he showed a little improvement. The man came every day for such treatments, but it was several weeks before he recovered fully. The man did not know what made him like that, but Pak Tunjung explained it was because he did not pray before the performance and was therefore vulnerable to "black magic."

Pak Tunjung emphasized to me that it was very important to always follow the proper procedures so that something similar would not happen to me. He demonstrated his meaning by using his fingers as a kind of puppet. He held up his left finger and said that was me, then he showed his right finger coming right at "me," as if to knock me over. Pak Tunjung said that if I was not protected by my skill and knowledge that the other finger, representing "black magic," would strike me and kill me. Pak Tunjung reassured me that because I continued to study and work hard, the "black magic" would just go around and not touch me. He illustrated this by showing the right finger coming at "me," but then veering off to the side and going around. Pak Tunjung said it was not my job to fight back or destroy the "black magic" but to just stay safe. The ability to "stay safe" requires knowledge and skill within a tradition.

My performance and the performance given by Ibu Suratni demonstrate how wayang kulit acts as ritual to function as social power in Balinese society based on the social identity of the dalang. A community demonstrates their power by selecting a performer who is well known or powerful. For example, for the ceremony to bless a new priest in Ubud, the most famous dalang, Cenk Blonk (I Wayan Nardayana), was invited to give a performance. He is well known for his comedy, and VCDs, radio programs, and television shows of his performances are common (he also has a considerable presence on YouTube). The power of the dalang, because he is a kind of superstar, would reflect back on the community who sponsored him. A woman dalang, therefore, might seem a weak choice for the ritual performance. Andrew N. Weintraub (2004, 83), in his work about wayang golek, notes three levels of discourse for understanding how a dalang functions in relation to society—(1)

the path to knowledge and familial relations; (2) skill, individuality, and the aesthetics of performance; (3) public status.

Ibu Suratni and I were both beholden to the men who taught us to perform wayang kulit. Neither of us was part of a familial line of dalang; we depended on teachers through the university and in the village for our craft. Our own work reflected back on our teachers, and their own reputation would rise or fall depending on the success or failure we had in performance. Our performances were granted the authority of our male teachers—it was their wisdom and talent that animated our puppets. State institutions grant power and authority to the performance of women dalang because they, for the most part, received their training there. Many performances by early women dalang were not for religious ceremony but rather were part of state-led competitions or showcases. Knowledge from both traditional and modern systems of knowledge transfer power and prestige to the artist (Anderson 1990, 54–58).

The skill of the dalang and his ability to manipulate the aesthetics of wayang kulit might be understood as charisma. Anderson (1990, 43) suggests that *charisma* is one of the key terms for understanding the Indonesian conception of power. Attracting a large audience is a visible demonstration of charisma and power. Ibu Suratni's performance was remarkable because people gathered around to watch—even though no one typically watches a wayang lemah performance. The presence of the audience also cast doubt on the efficacy of her performance as ritual. My audience included respected arts professors, whose approval enhanced the status of my performance. "Black magic" challenged my performance, suggesting the efficacy or power of my performance was also in doubt. As women, the signs of a charismatic performance were difficult to read or standardize. We functioned within and challenged the systems of power within the tradition of wayang kulit.

Finally, the public status of the performer determines the potential for social power within the event. Villages or families often spend large sums of money to hire a popular dalang, which then reflects back positively on the family or village. Ibu Suratni is a well-known performer in her village and is popular around the island because of her performances in other types of theater.[3] Also, there are very few women dalang in Bali.[4] By selecting Ibu Suratni, the villagers added prestige to the ceremony. As a foreigner and a woman my performance added prestige because of its novelty. Novelty is always highly regarded in Balinese performance and ceremony—I saw many additions or variations on "tradition" while in Bali, such as a performance by a woman dalang, but rarely do these novelties become the norm. These innovations must remain rare in order to maintain their power—if women performed often it would not have a high status.

At the same time, Ibu Suratni might have been picked out of necessity rather than prestige. The ceremony at which she performed was given by members of the village who needed to pool their money. They did not want to spend a large sum to hire a dalang for a wayang lemah performance, which is ritually important but not the focus of the event. By casting Ibu Suratni the committee saved money. A dalang who is a member of the community might not receive any payment if he does the performance as *ngayah* (ritual offering). Ibu Suratni told me, "The people in this area are happy; they do not need to go outside to find a dalang; there is one right here, someone who is part of their family." Likewise, I was not paid for my performance. Rather, I was the one who paid for the musicians and transportation so that I could perform. I did not have the same community obligation as Ibu Suratni, but the performance was done as a favor for one of Pak Tunjung's friends. Both Ibu Suratni and I were able to perform as part of a complex web of obligation, prestige, and power.

The arrangement helped Ibu Suratni as well. Ceremonies are expensive, and each member of the community (*banjar*) is required to contribute financially to the event. Many banjar had public lists posted of what each member was required to pay and whether the family was able to meet that obligation. If a family does not, they are publically shamed and can be ostracized.[5] Ibu Suratni's husband did not have a job at the time of this ceremony, and their large family struggled to survive on what Ibu Suratni earned as a performer—very few performers in Bali earn enough for that to be their sole income. Performing at the ceremony as ngayah would relieve her family of any financial obligation. In Bali I met several male dalang who performed wayang as a hobby, who served their community in this way. Performing at the ceremony helped my research and has added to my reputation as a performer and scholar both within and outside Bali. Gender complicates the relationship between power and tradition within and around our puppet performances.

Chapter 5

WOMEN DALANG

Negotiating the Invisible and Visible Realms

> *Only the "crazy" people have both the courage and*
> *capacity to challenge the establishment.*
> —Bali governor I Made Mangku Pastika[1]

Women dalang must be understood within the larger social contexts of Bali and Indonesia. Women in Bali experience limitations within a social context that ostensibly promises more: an amendment to the original Indonesian constitution guarantees equality for all citizens (Kaelan 2008, 280–81), which has led to expanded education and political involvement for women.[2] Even so, women in Bali experience oppression based primarily on a notion of duty, or *tugas,* which means that women and men have different responsibilities to their communities and families. Balinese society perceives gender primarily through a person's actions, and women's role in Balinese society was and still is mainly within the sphere of the home. Luh Ketut Suryani, a Balinese scholar and noted psychiatrist, writes, "In Bali, the primary female role is one of fostering balance and harmony within families." Women are expected to marry, produce children, and "work as part of a family team" (2004, 213). An important part of this teamwork consists of women making offerings, both simple and elaborate, to be used in daily or special ceremonies. Women typically awake before dawn to go to the market, work all day preparing meals and minding children, and then work late into the night creating offerings. These activities, or tugas, though important, do not carry much prestige or power within Balinese society (Susilo 2003, 9–12). A change in the differentiation of actions, such as women performing as dalang, points to a possible rift in the social order.

Women in Bali are expected to get married and have children—only married couples are recognized as full members of the local community, or banjar. Pak Tunjung, demonstrating some humor I might include in my performance, illustrated how strong this expectation is:

> TWALEN: Oh, I hate to go up the mountain for such a long time. It makes me think of my wife—maybe she will forget me while I am gone. You do not need to worry about that because you are not yet married. Why is that? I am concerned because you have taken so long to find a wife.

> MERDAH: Father, do not worry. I am still young and there is still plenty of time for me to get married. Right now, it is important for me to first study and work. After I graduate I can find a wife.

> TWALEN: But son, I am older than you and wiser. If you wait too long it will be too late and then what will you do?

> MERDAH: Father, I am too busy right now for a wife. Do not be concerned; there will be time for me to have a family later.

> TWALEN: OK, but do not forget. Once you have completed school it is very important for you to find a wife and be happy.

As Pak Tunjung performed this dialogue for me I felt that he was commenting on my choice not to be married. Even after he met my partner, Tina, he would often still express the hope that I might find a husband and have children. Many of the Balinese I met were very surprised that I do not have a husband and children, and Pak

Tunjung was no exception. Through Twalen and Merdah he was also able to express concern that I should not wait too long and that he hoped once I was done with school, I would get married and have children; however, he also expressed acceptance of my choice. It reminded me that no matter what my actions or what I am studying in Bali, I am always viewed first as a woman. They were happy to let me study their art, and they respected me as a scholar, but there was still the expectation that I would fulfill my obvious role in society—that I would get married and have children. If I felt this pressure, and if it influenced my work in Bali, I realized that it must be even more so for Balinese women.

Several Balinese with whom I spoke argued that women dalang were proof of gender equality, noting that there have been several successful women dalang. However, this trend has not flourished, as it has for women's participation in other Balinese performing arts such as gamelan or dance, where women performers are quite common. Some artists and community members in Bali question women's ability to undertake the difficult physical and spiritual tasks of performing wayang kulit. Balinese scholar I Dewa Ketut Wicaksana articulates common Balinese objections to women dalang:

> There are several obstacles that women dalang must face, such as their physicality and biology, achieving competence with the technique, ethical concerns, responsibilities to family and community, and the sacredness [sesucian] of the wayang. Physically, women are too weak to undertake the activities of a dalang [aktivitas ngwayang] in their entirety—bayu, sabda, idep [energy or power, voice, and thinking or intelligence], and women do not have the time to do these all at the same time. (2000, 88; my translation)

Physically not strong enough? Balinese women often perform arduous tasks as part of their daily routines. I have seen women carrying heavy loads of rocks for construction or baskets of rice.

Wicaksana concludes that women dalang must practice and perform wayang kulit carefully in order to remain what the Balinese
call "luh luhwih" (womanly women) and not become "luh luhu"
(women who are trash) (ibid.).

To appreciate the shift that women performing as dalang might
represent, one must comprehend how power and agency are ne-
gotiated and understood within a Balinese context. Women must
constantly position themselves within society's structures, and some
women may have more success finding power than others. This
individual agency does not necessarily indicate a shift within those
structures, because agency is not the same as power. Anthropologist Lyn Parker, doing research in Bali, has determined that agency
is generally short term, rooted in self-interest, and pragmatic. She
writes, "Given the conditions and contingencies under which most
women live their lives, agency may often be all that is possible"
(2005, 85–88), which suggests that these women's actions do not
effect greater social change. In an insightful study on girl's and
women's gamelan groups,[3] Sonja Lynn Downing (2010) applies the
concept of agency to gauge the level of choice the girls in her study
have in constructing their own gender identities. She focuses on
how individual women feel constrained by "appropriate behavior,"
lack of time, and other restrictions and how some women overcome
those obstacles in order to play in or even lead a gamelan group.
Downing's conclusions demonstrate how an individual might
navigate the complex elements of tradition and societal norms that
are part of the arts in Bali, but because agency is focused on the
individual, her study is not able to account for the different ways
gamelan functions in relation to larger social structures. At the end
of the article she admits that since "the embodiment of music and
gender and the balancing act of various influences happen over
time, there is room for individual negotiation and interaction with
others and one's environment" (2010, 76). My intention here is not
to discredit Downing's work but rather use it as an example of how
agency is a limiting concept for understanding the relationships
between gender, wayang kulit, and Balinese society, especially

because women dalang are such an anomaly in Balinese society. Women making advances within male spheres of Balinese society encounter a local discourse that often discredits their activity and therefore maintains the gender status quo—they must negotiate the binary between luh luhwih and luh luhu (womanly or trash). Rather than focusing on just agency, I will foreground the connection the women's actions have to the larger social sphere as a way to elucidate the connection between tradition and societal power.

The New Opportunity

In the past, Balinese women did not have the opportunity to study wayang kulit because the skills of a dalang were typically passed down from father to son. Occasionally a dalang might teach another boy from the village if he showed especially keen interest and aptitude, and that student would then become like a son to his teacher. A dalang would never teach a daughter, and women rarely had opportunities to watch the performances. In the past,[4] wayang kulit, even though it is a public art form, existed outside the usual social sphere for women in the society, and women were rarely, if ever, in the audience. Hobart, writing in the late 1980s, offers one explanation for this lack of interest:

> It is first relevant to recall that a night wayang primarily attracts adult men and boys of all ages. It rarely compels the interest or enthusiasm of females. This is in line with the complementary division of the sexes in Balinese society alluded to earlier. Although times are changing, men are ideally still considered responsible for the perpetuation of cultural heritage. Particularly as they grow older, men become increasingly concerned with philosophical, religious, and literary matters, and with acquiring verbal fluency. . . . In contrast, few intellectual demands were traditionally made on women. In the religious field they mainly had to know

how to make the offerings required for rites and festivals. Their duties were primarily in the private sphere of the household. (1987, 185)

My own field research, conducted more than twenty years after Hobart's, revealed that little had changed: women are rarely in the audience for a wayang kulit performance, nor do they participate in many other nighttime events. Laura Noszlopy, in her research on popular youth activities in Bali, found that young women faced dual restrictions on participating in evening activities. One is that they had little time: "Girls regularly complained of being over burdened with the practical duties entailed in religious obligations and often showed me how their fingers were scratched and raw from making offerings." The other is that girls are rarely out after dark, and that those who do go out at night are often subjected to scorn and ridicule from boys and young men (2005, 186). In order for women to become dalang, a different path to the art is required.

A more recent alternative, since the mid-1970s, has been to study wayang kulit at state-sponsored schools for the arts.[5] This course of study, called *pedalangan* (arts of a dalang), introduces student dalang to different styles and teaches them a few basic stories. This opportunity allows those students, including women, who otherwise might have neither access nor exposure to the art form to study it and gain a recognized credential. The training provided at these arts schools offered the first key opportunity for women, such as Ni Ketut Trijata and Ni Wayan Rasiani, to become dalang.

Ni Ketut Trijata is often acknowledged as the first Balinese woman dalang (fig. 5.1). She currently lives in the area of Tabanan with her husband and daughters. Ibu Trijata studied pedalangan at both the high school and college levels and now teaches dance and Balinese language at a local high school and within the village. If there are students who desire to learn pedalangan, she will teach it as an extra course, but she admitted such opportunities are rare. Ibu Trijata gave her first performance in 1977, and as she gained recognition as a dalang, she had other invitations to perform both

Figure 5.1. Ni Ketut Trijata holds two of her favorite puppets. *Photo by author.*

wayang peteng and *wayang lemah* (night and day wayang, respectively). Ibu Trijata said she still performs occasionally for local events near her home but is better known for her performances in dance dramas such as arja.[6]

Ni Wayan Rasiani is one of the other early women dalang (fig. 5.2). She was originally from the village of Tabanan but now lives

Figure 5.2. Ni Wayan Rasiani and the author. *Photo by Ni Made Murniarti.*

in Denpasar. Ibu Rasiani studied wayang kulit at the high school level and did her first performance at a family celebration. She rarely performs but currently works as a teacher in the pedalangan program at SMKI, the Balinese high school for the arts. Together, the experiences of Ibu Trijata and Ibu Rasiani provide insight into this early opportunity for women and how power functions through their training and subsequent identities as dalang.

Both Ibu Trijata and Ibu Rasiani received the chance to become dalang because of an initiative undertaken by I Nyoman Suman-dhi, the then head of the Performing Arts High School (Sekolah Menengah Kesenian Indonesia, SMKI) and a longtime member of the steering committee for the Bali Arts Festival (Pesta Kesenian Bali, PKB). Kathy Foley, a noted scholar of Indonesian performing arts and Southeast Asian puppetry, in an interview with Sumandhi, asked how these women began to practice and why the PKB was committed to giving them an opportunity. Sumandhi replied that Foley and other Americans who had studied wayang kulit with him in the early 1970s prompted him to teach Balinese women: "I just wanted to give females a chance. I wanted to have women participate, because in America girls could study *wayang*" (Sumandhi 1994, 285). He wanted to use wayang kulit as a platform to demonstrate that women in Indonesian arts have the same opportunities to perform male genres as women in other countries such as the United States.[7]

Ibu Trijata was exposed to wayang kulit from an early age but had no interest in becoming a dalang: "When I began at the SMKI, I did not want to study pedalangan, because in Bali there were no women dalang yet. Women were not brave enough to use the wayang—to touch them. They are sacred!" Therefore, when her uncle Pak Sumandhi approached her in 1975 about studying pedalangan, she was hesitant at first: "Pak Sumandhi said I should study it, but I did not want to. But there had never been a woman dalang. I had to be brave all by myself. So I tried." In 1977 she performed wayang kulit for an audience—her first performance was likely the first time a woman performed wayang kulit in Bali.

During the summer of 2011, I spoke with Pak Sumandhi about his niece and her first performance. Usually, beginning students learn the story Arjuna Tapa (Arjuna's meditation), in which Arjuna seeks wisdom at the top of the mountain Indra Kila Giri (see chapter 2 for more details). It is a good first story because it features some of the most basic character types in wayang kulit, has a simple plot, and the fight sequence is easier than most to execute. It is the same story I enacted for my first performance.

During Ibu Trijata's early training, however, Pak Sumandhi felt she was not able to adequately perform the voice and movements for the ogre Momosimoko. He worried that her voice was too soft and gentle to match the kasar, or rough, appearance of the puppet character. Additionally, Pak Sumandhi worried that the fight sequence might be too vigorous for her to execute well in performance. So in consultation with the dalang who was overseeing her training, they decided to have her learn another story instead. Pak Sumandhi could not remember exactly which story she learned, but that it was one with only alus characters and female puppets, such as the marriage of Draupadi. They preferred this choice because Ibu Trijata would not have to perform the more difficult, or kasar, voices and the story did not require a prolonged fight scene. Her gender, and its perceived limitations, determined for Pak Sumandhi the range she could have as a dalang and how the audience received her work. My own gender was a constant concern for my teacher, Pak Tunjung—he often explained that he taught me only the simple fight sequences because that "was enough for a woman." So much prestige and pressure are placed on the teacher to have a successful student that he will usually ensure success by teaching only simple characters and movements.

Ibu Trijata broke the initial barrier between women and pedalangan, and her success inspired other women to study the art form. One such woman, Ibu Rasiani, told me she had loved wayang kulit since she was little, but she acknowledged her experience was not common for a daughter. When she was young, she loved to spend her free time doing or watching art. She was able to watch many different kinds of performances because her father was a well-known dalang and an arja dancer:

> When I was little—I really liked to go to performances with my parents. I liked to watch wayang kulit. There were no women dalang then. I was never afraid to go to performances, even at night. You had to be careful coming home because it was so dark and you might fall. In the wayang performances there were many symbols, like those of god. During every performance I would be happy because there was so much emotion in a wayang performance—expressed in the voice, like crying. Stories were not as funny as they are now. When I was a kid, women and girls would usually have to go straight home after school to help their mothers in the home. But I was different. I could go see my father perform and he would tell me the traditional stories. It was like a hobby for me, to listen to and tell the stories of dalang. I also studied dance—not just wayang. I learned the basics,

like how to be appropriate and clear [*cocok dan jelas*] for both. It was a hobby of mine to play wayang.

Ibu Trijata acknowledges she was "different," because, like a son, she had early exposure to the art form, which was remarkable because women and especially girls were rarely allowed to go to the late-night wayang performances. Inspired by this early experience, she even began to study wayang kulit at home with her father, and commented, "That is only natural, right?" When she went to the SMKI, Pak Sumandhi then also urged her to study pedalangan.

Ibu Rasiani frames her study of wayang kulit rather differently:

> AUTHOR: Usually only men can become dalang, so why did you want to become a dalang? Can women now become dalang?

> IBU RASIANI: I tried and became a dalang but it is rare, because although I think that women also can join in with men like that, it is still a big thing. For example, a girl must think, "Why can't I?" I tried and then I was able to do it. Now I work at the SMKI. I teach pedalangan. Maybe if I had picked a different major I would not be a teacher now.

> AUTHOR: Is wayang kulit performed by a woman different or the same as performed by a man? How and why?

> IBU RASIANI: Different? It is the same, because men and women both study the same thing, although it is rare for a woman to become a dalang. But both have to follow the same structure of performance. Women do have a boundary [*kerbatasan*] here. I see performances by men and they are freer. Women are more limited because of their ethics; they do not feel as free to be creative. But when I was a student, I had a big voice and did not feel very limited. But for women the voice is hard. It is hard to really compare.

Ibu Rasiani's comments reflect the complex nature of women performing. She states that women are able to perform just like men, but she immediately qualifies the statement. Women are breaking several social norms when they perform, for one, they are not sitting in a position considered polite for a woman. Secondly, Ibu Rasiani acknowledges she uses a "big voice," and thus in order to perform as a dalang she must use a voice not considered appropriate for a woman.

Ibu Rasiani acknowledges that she is breaking cultural boundaries in her performance, and likewise she found that some people felt she should not be a dalang because it would get in the way of her fulfilling her societal role (tugas) as a woman. She commented, "Before I got married, my husband already knew that I did wayang kulit. That it was my job. When I first did wayang kulit others thought that maybe it would be a problem for me to find a husband and have a family." Ibu Rasiani did not encounter that problem, but she consciously positions her involvement in wayang kulit as a hobby, and this points to an awareness that she needed to be careful to find an appropriate role as a "woman" dalang: "I did not do commercial wayang, I studied the academic side of things and wanted to teach. I did not feel it was a problem to do that and to get married." She told me that other girls did not want to study pedalangan because they felt they would not be able to get a husband and that studying wayang kulit was inappropriate for a woman.

The state-sponsored arts schools that provided both Ibu Trijata and Ibu Rasiani with their training and opportunity offer a very different training environment for a would-be dalang than he or she would experience in the village. I Nyoman Sedana, a Balinese scholar and dalang who is a professor at ISI describes the training given within the school system. At the high school level, students take many classes outside their primary focus, such as the philosophy of Pancasila, physical education, religion, Indonesian language, history, economics, and English. The pedalangan program includes classes in Balinese language and literature, performance theory, dance, voice, and practicum in performance. Each year at the university, students continue that wide range of study, but students also focus on a particular story taught by one teacher as a way to introduce that style of performance. In the village, a student training to be a dalang would have deeper exposure to one style, and theory would be combined with practice (Sedana 1993, 16–19). Students at the university are required to compose their own performance at the end of their training as a type of thesis before graduating.

The arts university provides many advantages but is also limiting in its scope. Sedana notes that dalang who rely primarily on the state system for their training and did not come to the school with a foundation of village training are not able to learn enough in order to make a living as a dalang. Those with previous experience and training as dalang are the most successful graduates of the program. These students seek the degree primarily as an official credential that will allow them to teach at a school or work in a government office as a supplement to work as a dalang (Sedana 1993, 29–31). If women must rely on ISI as their primary, or only, entry into the tradition, it inherently limits their ability because the school does not provide its students with the comprehensive skills, knowledge, or materials necessary to perform as a dalang.

Unlike the women in the program, most of the male student dalang had undergone training within their family line of dalang, and the skills and physical objects of the trade are passed down from father to son. Thus a male dalang is likely to have puppets that have served for several generations and therefore have accumulated a larger amount of taksu, or spiritual power. A dalang who does not come from a performing family must purchase the puppets, box, gender wayang, oil lamp, and screen; a rather large expense that causes many students at ISI to change their major (Sedana 1993, 26). Most of the women I interviewed did not have a full set of puppets and often had to borrow them from someone in order to perform. Pak Sumandhi mentioned in conversation with me that as part of the initial initiative to help women dalang the government would provide money so that women like Ibu Trijata could purchase some puppets, but she still did not have a very full set. Puppets purchased in this way would also not have the accumulated taksu and reputation from generations of performances. Pak Tunjung made many of my puppets for me, and I even assisted in making some of them by carving the simpler parts of the design. I purchased other puppets from Pak Artwa. Pak Tunjung also gave me some of the puppets from his own collection—a few of them were more than one generation old. He felt these puppets would give my performance greater authority and strength.

Male dalang also have greater access to giving performances because often, if their teacher cannot give a performance, he will send a student in his place. Women, because the majority of them received their training within the universities, do not have access to this social network.

The context of government sponsorship allowed women to break the "rules" because it created a place to study and create art outside the "tradition." Anthropologist Brett Hough (1999, 236–37), in his study of the programs at the arts university in Bali, recognizes the tension between state ideals and local norms by splitting Balinese culture into two domains: there is the official domain, which informs policy decisions, and the autonomous domain, which is local identity, language, and values. Schools such as ISI exist as sites of tension between these two cultural domains. On one hand the schools are run by the state (for example the *rektor,* or university president, is ultimately appointed by a committee in Jakarta, and much of the curriculum comes from Javanese models as well) and adhere to state ideologies. On the other hand these same schools teach local arts and traditions to a mostly local population of students. Hough notes that the primary goal of the education system is to develop a national culture because it forms the basis of a culture that will foster modernity and development (237–39). Curriculum in the schools is set by officials in Jakarta—thus the emphasis on creating an innovative performance for a final thesis project rather than performing a traditional wayang. A woman studying and graduating with a degree in wayang kulit is but one example of this mixing of state initiatives and local culture. Since the religious aspect that is inherent in traditional training is not prioritized, the students emerging from the school, while technically proficient, will, in theory, remain secular dalang and not exercise the full range of the form. However, in practice this is not really the case. In spite of the stated intention and structure of the arts training at ISI, the different performing arts are never completely separated from their religious and spiritual intent.

Sumandhi, together with the school he represents, desired to separate the process of learning wayang kulit from performing it as a part of ritual, a connection that is really an intrinsic part of wayang. Hobart states that wayang is always "instructive, entertaining, and religious in intent" (1987, 172). In response to this concern, Foley, in her interview, asked, "Would anyone teach the female dalang to do ritual performance?" to which Sumandhi replied, "That is up to their own village. Since the customs for ritual performances differ from one area to the next, we do not teach that material in the arts schools. Students must study it on their own" (Sumandhi 1994, 284). For a dalang to be able to perform, it is generally expected that he or she be able to practice the ritual side of performance, and, if a dalang is dependent solely on the school program for education and has not undergone the ritual preparation and training, his or her opportunities to perform would be extremely limited (Sedana 1993, 21, 32–34).

Most of the women dalang I spoke with, or heard about, performed in both secular and sacred contexts, which implies a completion of ritual training.[8] The initial opportunity, sanctioned by the school and government, carried its own sense of power because of the women's association with a powerful entity. Errington (1990) claims that power and potency in Indonesia are accumulative—they develop and increase over time—and that power also accrues through association. That is why having the PKB or university sponsor women performers gives the women more power in their performance, but this is secular power and not spiritual power, which is also important in Bali. Women, once given the opportunity to study pedalangan, often continue to study with another dalang in the village. They give performances in a variety of contexts and undergo the ritual initiation that gave them access to spiritual power as well. The program at the schools and Sumandhi's initial initiative does not directly interact with the spiritual/ritual realm, which is important to wayang kulit. I do not intend to conflate one with the other; even so, for the women, like most other pedalangan students, a connection was forged that created a platform for power as dalang within the community. The dalang trained at the university have power not only because of the credential but also because of the inherent spiritual power expressed by a dalang in a wayang kulit performance.

Outside the University

Ni Wayan Nondri (fig. 5.3) is a woman dalang who trained outside the university and thus had unique opportunities that propelled her to be generally known as the best and most accomplished of all the women dalang. She grew up watching her father perform, and after her husband, I Ketut Madra (a popular dalang from Su-kuwati), died in a traffic accident in 1979, she began performing wayang kulit three months later in order to support her family. The first time I met Ibu Nondri was in the art market at Sukowati, a village not far from Ubud known for its arts and crafts. Both Balinese and tourists come here to shop and buy a variety of items for the home or souvenirs—it is a busy, sprawling center of activity. Ibu Nondri worked at a small stall selling candy, cigarettes, snacks, and drinks. She was a small, frail-looking old woman, but her eyes were expressive and energetic. She wore a sarong and T-shirt, with her white hair pulled back into a loose bun. I explained that I was doing research on wayang kulit and would like to interview her.

Figure 5.3. Ni Wayan Nondri and the author. *Photo by Ni Made Murniarti.*

Ibu Nondri smiled and told me to come the next night around seven o'clock, after she got home from work.

Ibu Nondri was born only a few houses away from where she currently lives. She got married in 1972 and had three sons, who still live close to her. Two live in the same compound and the third lives next door.[9] When Ibu Nondri was little she often had to help her parents around the house, but when she had time she liked to play and pretend she was putting on performances where she would tell stories from the wayang. Her father was a dalang, but he died when he was thirty, while she was still a young girl. She did not go to school for art but like most girls she studied dance in the village and she told me that her favorite was *tarian parawa,* the dances that tell the stories from the Mahabharata. She explained, "It is a dance that tells the stories of the wayang. I think it is a good dance for someone to do before studying wayang." The dance gave her familiarity with the stories and characters she would later perform in wayang.

It was soon after the birth of her third child that her husband died, and at that moment Ibu Nondri decided to become a dalang:

> After my husband died, I felt I must study how to do wayang. I felt what else could I do? After my husband died I did not have any work to do. It was before I sold things in the market. When he was alive, I liked to stay up with him and watch him play with the wayang and read stories. I helped him create stories. As soon as the children fell asleep I would help him make stories. But then he died. I then took my own initiative to study wayang. Since I was little, the stories and the puppets made me happy. It was like I was married to all things wayang [mekekawin].

She studied with her brother, I Wayan Wija, who was already an accomplished dalang, and worked on her skills every day after her children went to bed.

> After I was done with the work around the house—I had taken care of the children and prepared the food in the kitchen—sometimes I would then take a book and read a little. Every night when everyone slept I would rehearse. I would have to practice how to move the wayang. It was really difficult! The dalang in Bali, especially Sukuwati, must be able to move their foot to make percussion as well as use their arms and hands, and their voice. I had to study every day and every night.

Her husband died in January, and she gave her first performance in May. Her ability to so quickly master the skills of a dalang demonstrates how important early exposure is for women dalang.

Ibu Nondri acknowledged that watching and participating in the wayang was not normal for a daughter or wife, but these opportunities gave her access to the taksu she would need to give a performance. She did not think there was that much of a difference between a man and woman dalang; however, she did say,

> Yeah, I think it is harder for women, because once a month women menstruate and they may not perform then. I always had to try to adjust my performance schedule around my menstruation [she laughed], because when I had my period I could not go out. I tried to find a doctor to help, but during that time I was not brave enough to perform. It is OK to rehearse, but I was not brave enough to use the puppets. You may not touch them during that time.

Women in Bali are considered polluted during the period of their menstruation and they may not go to temple or handle offerings. Lene Pedersen (2002, 303–4) describes how menstrual taboos proscribed a dual identity upon women as both *sebel,* or "polluted," and *raja,* or "queen." During menstruation, women are prohibited from entering the temple or participating in ritual activities. Depending on caste, and the particularities of a woman's village or family, she might also be secluded and not allowed to wash, cook food, or clean. Sebel women are thought to attract the attention of the *bhuta kala,* or troublesome spirits, and to threaten the general and spiritual good of the community. In contrast, some women refer to their period as a time when they are "like a raja," because it gave them a rare break from the daily work of both the house and temple. Menstrual blood also possesses magic qualities and can be used to create either love charms or dangerous spells.

For a woman dalang, menstruation means she has to cancel a performance because she cannot go into the temple or touch the puppets during this time. Because today women can suppress the signs of menstruation, the threat always exists that a woman will proceed anyway, thus offending the gods and exposing the community to danger. Pedersen (2002, 308–9) confirms that women would sometimes lie about menstruation or hide it in order to participate in activities that they wanted to do. I observed that women were sometimes required to indicate the invisible state of menstruation with an outside symbol in order to alleviate anxiety. For example, my dance teacher wore a red ribbon on her kabaya at a dance performance outside a temple, indicating that she was menstruating and therefore would not go inside.

Even when not bleeding, Pedersen notes that women between menarche and menopause are not allowed to handle spiritually dangerous things such as a *keris,* or dagger. This same prohibition is extended to the puppets, and many of the women dalang I spoke with were extremely hesitant to touch the puppets when they began their training because it had been forbidden in the past. I Nyoman Sedana demonstrates how menstruation remains a primary concern:

> The first internal problem is due to [a woman dalang's] monthly menstruation that prohibits her to enter a holy place or space, to touch holy objects or wayang, to recite mantras or holy names and passages, and to perform any holy activities. The problem increases after the ritual offerings and foods have been delivered and consumed by the artists but the expected woman puppeteer suddenly got menstruation, which forced her to apologetically cancel the show at the last minute. Then the external problems and challenges start spreading out: who, where, and how to get a last-minute puppeteer to perform in lieu of the first for the noncancelable ritual ceremony. (pers. comm., November 1, 2013)

Ibu Nondri performed more often than the other women dalang; both at temples and for tourists, sometimes four times a week and occasionally only three or four times a month. She explained, "As long as I was able to fill my kitchen, that was enough." During my interview, she also referred to her performance as a hobby, but it was also clear that she performed as a dalang to support her family. She exclaimed, "Well, like a boy I wanted to become a dalang since I was very little. It was a hobby—but I did it so I could make money. That was my main reason!" She explained her family was happy with her decision to become a dalang so that she could support her children.

I asked Ibu Nondri if she thought that wayang kulit was different with a woman dalang, "is it still traditional wayang kulit?" Ibu Nondri exclaimed,

> Oh, it is the same. What would the purpose be of it being different? Why would it be different? The story is the same, the puppets move the same, and the voice is the same. The only difference is that women cannot perform during menstruation. Men do not have to worry about that.

Like the other women dalang I spoke with, Ibu Nondri locates the tradition of wayang kulit in the objects, context, and stories and not in the person doing the action. I wondered if she ever thought about what her husband's reaction might be to her performance. "Do you think a woman dalang would have a hard time finding a husband?" I asked. "No, it would not be a problem," she said, "everyone is free to make his or her own decisions. But I waited until after I was married to study to become a dalang. But then I was really happy that my brother had studied to be a dalang, because when he studied to become a dalang I would always watch and practice. It meant I could become a dalang very quickly." Ibu Nondri thought that her audiences were pleased with her performances and that they did not mind that she was a woman dalang. She laughed, "If they did not like it, they wouldn't have invited me back to perform at the next ceremony."

Many of the male dalang from Nondri's generation are still quite active, such as I Wayan Nartha and her brother Wija, so I asked Ibu Nondri if she still gave performances, and she sighed, "I am too old. I cannot perform anymore. You have to be so strong. I did perform at the arts festival a year or so ago, but that was the last time. It was only for two hours; before that I would perform for three or four hours. I was strong." Nondri explains that she does not perform any more because of her age, but I wonder whether that is the complete truth. She still works all day in the market. Instead, I think one reason she no longer performs is so that her sons might have the opportunity. Perhaps it is only appropriate for a woman to be a dalang when there is no one else to fill the role, but once there is, she is encouraged more than a man might be to step down.

Ibu Nondri was able to gain power in the performance because of her relationship to her family; the power accrued across the generations, and consent was given posthumously by her husband in a dream. This kind of blessing and guidance through a dream is common in Bali. I Made Bandem, scholar and performer, told me that he often dreamed of his father or one of his teachers when he was studying topeng or gambuh: "I need inspiration. A dream is also an imagination, which helped to raise my creativity in performance. Even now before performing, I often dream of my late father I Made Kredek, and I believe he brings me taksu" (Bandem 2015, pers. comm.). Ibu Nondri's performance was given approval and strength directly from her husband—and that this story circulates around the village gives credibility to her work as a dalang.

Another example of how family relates to power is Megawati Sukarnoputri, who became the fifth president of Indonesia on July 23, 2001. As with a woman dalang there was much debate about whether such a leadership role was appropriate for a woman,[10] but this time the scale was national. Much of this criticism focused on her lack of personality and her inability as a dynamic public speaker. Indonesian scholar Krishna Sen writes that there was, "a constant elision between Mega's silence and her lack of leadership capacity" (2002, 16–17). In order to be accepted as president, Megawati needed to balance being a strong leader together with Indonesian expectations of how a "proper" woman should behave. In her research on women's topeng in Bali, Carmencita Palermo found that several women cited etika as a major stumbling block in performing male characters. Women must follow kodrat, or the proper behavior for women, which requires them to be passive, quiet, and refined. Palermo found that "those who do not follow these unspoken rules are considered not normal" (2009, 12).

Evidence that Mega failed can be seen in her lost election bid in 2009. The possibility of both Ibu Nondri's and Megawati's success and then subsequent "failure" is tied to how power is accrued and realized in Balinese and Javanese society.[11] Megawati is the daughter of Indonesia's first president, Sukarno, just as Ibu Nondri is the daughter of a dalang. Spiritual and political potency then was able to accrue from father to daughter, and sometimes husband, along with the practical means and experience to succeed. The effects were not long lasting, however; once an appropriate male, like a son or another politician, was able to step into the leadership role the women were prompted to step aside. Power and spiritual potency are only available to women like Ibu Nondri and Megawati, and then on a limited basis and for a limited time.

The Same but Different

There are not many women currently studying to be dalang in the programs at ISI or even the SMKI, although there are several women studying in the pedalangan program. Many of the women in the program are able to go for only a few years and then drop out after marriage. Other women enter the program with no intention of becoming dalang; rather, they chose this course of study because it opens up very different opportunities for them as performers. One Balinese woman entertainer, Ni Nyoman Tjandri,[12] applied her study of the art of wayang kulit to become a very well known stage performer (fig. 5.4). Her choices and path as a dalang demonstrate how women studying wayang kulit renegotiate that opportunity on their own terms. Women like Ibu Tjandri do not want to become *like* male dalang but rather use the training as part of their own dynamic artistry.

I read about Ibu Tjandri before I met her. She has toured extensively internationally and performs as a dancer with Odin Teatret.[13] Her father was the well-known dancer I Made Kredek. She is best known for playing the condong role, or comic servant to the queen, in arja and has performed the comic roles for topeng with the all-women

Figure 5.4. Ni Nyoman Tjandri. *Photo by author.*

group Topeng Shakti. Ibu Tjandri is better known for these theatrical performances than as a dalang. Currently she lives outside Denpasar with her husband and members of her extended family.

At the beginning of our interview, after I explained my purpose and the topic of my research, Ibu Tjandri apologized, "Right now I am not really a dalang. I can only do it a little; I am not that smart with it. I work more as a dancer for arja or like that." I reassured her that I was interested in whatever she could tell me. Ibu Tjandri might not perform often or even identify as a dalang, but hers was the name most often mentioned when I asked other Balinese about women dalang. As I interviewed her, however, I noted a discrepancy between this public image and reality. Perhaps this demonstrates that many Balinese are more comfortable with a woman dalang who is not really a dalang, and her ambivalence might enhance her status rather than detract from it because she is not really challenging the social hierarchy but instead functions as an appropriate symbol for gender equality within the society.[14]

Ibu Tjandri began studying wayang kulit because she wanted to learn Kawi, an important language for many Balinese performance genres:

> After my dad died I studied Kawi. I thought maybe I would just study the language. But my teachers in Sukowati felt I should study the practical aspects of performance as well, like the practice of wayang. So that is why I studied wayang. I studied the different voices for Twalen, Merdah, Sangut, and Delem. Big voices and little voices. Before, I thought I would only study Kawi—but once I started they had me learning the voice for Arjuna and for the raksasa. I thought then I should maybe try a performance. I studied for three months and had a performance.

Three months may not seem like a long time to study before giving a performance, but it is one of the longest times I found in my research. Child dalang I Made Tangkas Harta Wiguna describes that he "has only been studying the art of shadow puppetry for one month," in preparation for a performance at the PKB (*Bali Daily,* June 6, 2012). Based on such statements, coupled with my own knowledge of how dalang are trained in Bali, it seems that there are many activities falling outside the formal preparation for a performance and that young dalang actually study, practice, and are exposed to the art form for many years. With that in mind, three months is a rather long time for focused "study" before giving a first performance. In comparison,

Ibu Nondri studied only one month, which demonstrates the importance of having early access to the art form through fathers, brothers, or husbands. Ibu Nondri had a similar support network and Ibu Tjandri did not; likewise Ibu Nondri is generally considered a better dalang than Ibu Tjandri. The complex relationship between the traditional art form and power within society is revealed when taking in account that, overall, Ibu Tjandri has enjoyed a longer career and more acclaim as a performer. Her work as a dalang, though limited, adds to her aura as an artist.

Ibu Tjandri enjoyed studying wayang kulit because it expanded her range as a performer: "You must be able to be both alus and kasar. Wayang has so many things, so many shadows. You have to make the raksasa so kasar." The word she used for shadows, *bayangan*, translates as both "shadow" and "imagination" and thus indicates the combination of physical, mental, and spiritual realms used in performance. Wayang kulit is unique because it provides a means for a human, in this case the dalang, to act in both the spiritual and physical realms, and that gives the dalang a powerful public voice.

Ibu Tjandri did not, or was not able to, use her dalang training to gain power in the same way a man would have access to it through a public voice. Instead, she used her training as a springboard for other performance genres:

> I like all the different characters. They are all different. If you want a big voice, you have a raksasa, or a small voice like Arjuna. It must be like that. Maybe it is easier for women to do the *manis* [sweet] voice, but you must study the other voices too. [She demonstrated the deep laugh of a raksasa voice] You need to study like that until your [own] voice disappears! Your voice must come from inside. But then your voice might not be good for singing . . . but then it comes back. It gets stronger. Before, I could do it better, but now it makes me cough.

Female characters in many of other genres of Balinese performance are often passive; they are not the dynamic or interesting elements within the story. Women rarely perform kasar characters in other forms of drama or dance, and performing wayang kulit provides a rare opportunity to use a kasar voice and to embody those dynamic characters. The female character that Ibu Tjandri is famous for, the condong,[15] is an exception. Ibu Tjandri explained the connection between wayang kulit and her success: "Because of my study in pedalangan, when I perform arja, I feel braver and smarter."

Ibu Tjandri has had to refashion her participation in a "male" art in order to make it acceptable for her as a woman artist and performer. There is a general discourse about women and the arts in Bali that accounts for the ability of women to participate in these kinds of art forms but argues that they must find a way to do so that is still distinctly female. In a conversation with music ethnologist Michael B. Bakan, I Wayan Dibia, a renowned Balinese and international performer, scholar, and teacher, shares his own opinion about women performers:

> I would reject the idea of women [dalang] making groaning and grunting vocal sounds [like those made by male dalang]. The woman dalang should explore the high voice, what is distinctive about a woman [performing in that context]. You have to give them more space to demonstrate what is special about women. This is why I reject the idea of developing women's *beleganjur*. (Bakan 1998, 475)

Beleganjur is a type of marching gamelan that descends from warrior dances, and like wayang kulit, it is beginning to be performed by women. Dibia goes on to explain that if women want to perform a "male" genre like wayang kulit or beleganjur, they should find a specifically feminine way of performing: "If it has to develop at all, it should be developing as something different that allows for the cultural expression of women to emerge" (ibid.). Dibia suggests that a woman should "feminize" the performance, much like Ibu Trijata's teachers when they taught her a story with few raksasa, but Tjandri's experience suggests another way. I believe that by appropriating the training available through wayang kulit but applying it to other genres, women such as Ibu Tjandri are empowering themselves as performers, even if they finally are best known for their work in genres other than wayang kulit. That Ibu Tjandri emerges as the most often named woman dalang speaks to the success she has had with this approach.

Ibu Tjandri is not the only woman dalang to use her training in order to develop skills that transfer to notable careers in other genres of performance. Ni Wayan Suratni (fig. 5.5), like Ibu Tjandri, is a very well known performer for her outrageous comic characters

Figure 5.5. Ni Wayan Suratni. *Photo by author.*

in *drama gong,* arja, and others. She was thirty-seven years old and the youngest woman dalang that I interviewed. She lived with her husband and three children; the youngest was still in preschool and sat with us during the interview. Her success as a performer is dependent on her ability to manage her family commitments while training, traveling, and performing.

Ibu Suratni could not remember the first time she saw wayang kulit because she went to many different kinds of performances when she was young. She began her study of wayang kulit with a dalang in her village, I Wayan Sidja, and then continued at ISI in 2000. She was already married when she began her study and explained that she needed to get permission from her family.

During her studies at the university, she gave birth to two of her children, and she complained that it was difficult to balance the needs of her family and make it to campus to attend lectures. Ibu Suratni also studied topeng at ISI (she completed the entire program in four semesters) and performed as a dancer and comedian. I wondered how she managed to find time to do all these things and be able to care for her family.

> IBU SURATNI: I had my family at my side. After I
> finished all my work here at home, then I could start
> to study, to practice. It is like that in Bali; if you are an
> artist you are always very busy. And then there were
> *upacara* [ceremonies] as well and lectures on campus.
> If I had a performance at night, I would get home
> very late but get up at five in the morning to make
> offerings. At 7:00 a.m. I would go to campus and finish
> there at noon. I would bring my costumes along with
> me and then go to give a performance at 1:00 p.m. To
> do this I had to change my clothes at campus right
> after the lecture and go directly there. Like I might
> perform for a wedding. After that, maybe I would not
> go right home; I would go to another performance
> before coming home. Then I might come home for
> a little bit before going to a performance that night.

I would stop at the temple to pray and then go dance *prembon*. Then, maybe starting at 10:00 p.m., I would have a drama gong performance. I would get home at 3:00 a.m. and then finally see my husband; I would get up the next day at 5:00 a.m. again. On the weekend I could sometimes sleep until 11:00 a.m., but as soon as it was morning my eyes would open and my mind would start working. I could not get back to sleep! I must get up. It was always like that! Although then sometimes I would take a nap later in the afternoon.

AUTHOR: And does your family help you? Does your husband help you with everything?

IBU SURATNI: Yes. If I have to go and I can only get a little bit done at home, my husband will help. The children already know how to do some cleaning and they help a little bit. But before I go, I have to make the offerings, but he will put the offerings out. Whenever I go out he stays with the children.

Her husband was not currently employed, so the family depended on Ibu Suratni's income from performing. He seemed very proud of his talented wife, but I sensed she was a bit frustrated that he did not work more in or out of the home. I often observed this tension between wives and husbands in Balinese households. Ibu Suratni revealed her attitude about this when I asked if it was harder for her to become a dalang because she was a woman:

No. But you must have a strong commitment. You need to study together with the other students on campus and study at home. You need to work on your voice and on the movement of the puppets. Sometimes the men are lazy [*malas*]; however, men are more capable [*mampu*] than women. However, I think if a woman wants to do something, she definitely can, because women work so hard.

Seemingly, the men could choose to work or not, and they could choose to help around the house or not, but the wife had to do these things. I asked her if she thought there was equality between the genders:

> Oh, for sure it is still very different! Men do not have to have children, they do not have to take care of the home. They are able to go out more and do more things. Right now women still have to do a lot of things. For example, if a child is sick, that has to come first. A woman might be late then, going to the pura to dance, pray, or give offerings.

She sighed, "Maybe later it will get better and women will have more equality with men."

Ibu Suratni also expressed dissatisfaction with the limited training at ISI:

> The lessons at campus allowed for only a little bit of work with the puppets. You did not learn as much, so I kept studying with Pak Sidja. After lecture I would go right there to practice what I learned. If I wanted to complete my education in wayang kulit, I needed to practice with the music.

Her family and teachers were really happy to help her and did not think it was strange that she wanted to learn wayang kulit. Pak Sidja felt that if someone was willing to come (*pasti akan dia ajar*), for sure he would teach her. When Ibu Suratni confirmed, "I am brave [*berani*]," she was acknowledging how difficult it was and is to become a dalang and to perform when her family lineage and gender position her outside the tradition. She was dependent on the university and the kindness of a local dalang for her training and this limited her scope as a performer.

This frustration could be sensed when Ibu Suratni shared the other women's feelings that the voice of a woman dalang was different from a man's: "the voice of a woman always appears like that of a woman, a woman dalang." She felt that men have a natural ability to speak in a deep voice and do not need to spend as much time rehearsing it. She told me about how she practiced her voice every day, even practicing out in the rain. Finally, she felt, "I am capable. I can do the voice of Dimbi [Bima's wife]. I can do the voices for *raksasa wanita* (female ogre characters). I can do it very good. I did that for my final exam at ISI." Then she demonstrated her voice for the clown characters of Twalen and Delem, and I thought her voice was as deep and gravelly as many men. The repeated exclamation, "I can do it. I am brave," reveals her willingness to break normative gender expectations through her performance. She does not perform wayang kulit differently than a man but rather negotiates the time and space of her performance to her own advantage. She is brave because she performs and claims her own place within the tradition.

At the end of our interview Ibu Suratni told me that in a week she would be giving a performance of wayang lemah for a village mass cremation and that I could come see the performance. She said she usually performed wayang about once a month. People asked her to perform more often, but she was so busy as a dancer that she usually had to turn down the invitation. Unlike most male dalang, she did not have a student that she could send in her place. Before I left I asked her about the responses she received from her family and community regarding her work as a dalang:

> IBU SURATNI: There are a lot of positive and negative comments; some people might not like it, but they do not tell me that. People who feel positive about it might telephone me and they give me support. People who are negative might feel, why did you become a dalang? People like that are not capable like me. I work hard and study. But I think that most people are supportive. The people in this area are happy that they do not need to go outside to find a dalang; there is one right here, someone who is part of their family.

AUTHOR: What advice would you have for a girl who might want to become a dalang?

IBU SURATNI: You have to be careful. Even right after having my children I had to get up after only a week. You have to transfer your energy. Both girls and boys can be smart at making dance or music. But if you have a feeling for making art, you have to be brave; you must be able to memorize music really quickly. Like one of my kids is studying arja because he likes to dance. It requires a lot of commitment; they must want to do it. If they want to do something else, that is OK. My children do not need to do just like me.

AUTHOR: Is there anything else you wanted to add?

IBU SURATNI: I think it is great that you are able to do this research, to get to know how things are for women in Bali. Things like that are important. Later I hope you will give me your book. I hope you have great success.

Women Dalang and Power

Discourses of national and local forces intertwine and compete with visible and invisible referents to power in the case of women dalang. Ibu Nondri drew from the power of her father and husband in order to be considered the "most successful woman dalang." Ibu Trijata and Ibu Rasiani were given their opportunity through a state-sponsored initiative but also depended on the support of their community in order to receive enough training and performance opportunities to hone their skill. That they both teach—Ibu Trijata in her community and Ibu Rasiani at the state-sponsored arts school—is a continuation of that initiative. Ibu Suratni and Ibu Tjandri manipulated the opportunity to study pedalangan into locally acceptable performance careers. Their training as dalang gives each woman special status even though they are better known for their performances in arja and other dramatic forms. Each of these five remarkable women have achieved much as artists and as dalang—but gender proved a barrier to accessing the kinds of power available to a male dalang. The aesthetics and practices of performance, together with discourses around ritual and spiritual power, remain gendered. These women demonstrate that women could be dalang, but the structures of society were not transformed by their actions.

Chapter 6

THOUGHTS FROM
THE SHADOWS

The story of Arjuna Tapa does not end with Arjuna's victory over the raksasa Momosimoko. After the battle, the god Indra appears on a golden chariot. Indra explains there is another, more powerful, raksasa, or ogre, causing havoc in the heavens. The raksasa's name is Niwatakwaca—and only Arjuna is capable of destroying this menace. Arjuna agrees to accompany Indra to the heavens in order to do battle. At this point in my performance of Arjuna Tapa, I would have the clown characters of Twalen and Merdah explain that the performance has ended for the night but that the great epic story continues on. I often ended with the promise that maybe someday I could return and perform this next part of the story, telling of the battle in heaven, for my audience, whether they were in Ohio, Michigan, or Indiana. Finally, during one of my return trips to Bali, Pak Tunjung agreed to teach me this second part of the story; it is called Gugur Niwatakwaca. Arjuna Tapa and Gugur Niwatakwaca are both part of Arjuna Wiwaha, one of the oldest representatives of old Javanese literature. Arjuna Wiwaha provides story material for many wayang kulit performances.[1]

Gugur Niwatakwaca features a strong female character—the heavenly nymph Suprabha—and several female comic characters—the *condong* and the *nenek*. The condong is a comic servant character who often accompanies the alus female character in many types of Balinese performing arts. The condong puppet is dark colored and bare chested; her gaze looks forward; and her sarong and hairstyle are both simple. Even though the condong is a comic character like Twalen, her mouth is not articulated and she rarely if ever serves to translate the Kawi language that alus characters speak into the local language. *Nenek* means grandmother, and this character has a broad mouth, a little nose, big gaping teeth, drooping breasts, and an awkwardly tied sarong. Remarkably, she has an articulated mouth, although like the condong, she does no translation. Learning a story with these women characters offered further insight into how performance might negotiate gender hierarchy and tradition.

Gugur Niwatakwaca, after the usual ritual opening of the kayonan dance and the entrance of the puppets, begins with a scene between Arjuna and Suprabha. The interactions between these two characters reveal archetypes of relationships between women and men in Bali. Suprabha, like the women dalang in my research, emerges as a possible hero and role model for women in Balinese society—but the story, as I learned it, also suggests that for even women heroes, like women dalang, the sphere of action remains limited by gender. Arjuna speaks first, in response to a question from Suprabha, that the audience does not hear. He explains that Indra arranged for their meeting because a giant raksasa, Niwatakwaca, is destroying the heavens. Indra wants Suprabha to accompany Arjuna to face this menace. The characters of Arjuna and Suprabha speak in Kawi and the penasar Twalen and Merdah translate the words into the local language for the audience. Next, Suprabha speaks—she protests that she is only a woman and therefore unable to help. "If a mighty ogre is so strong that even the gods cannot resist him, what can I, a woman, do?" Arjuna assures Suprabha that she has a special power because she is so beautiful, and "women with beauty hold a special power over men." Finally she agrees and the two travel up to heaven.

Beauty directly translates into spiritual and societal power for women. In Bali, "women have a religious obligation to beautify themselves for religious observances," and for women especially, the performing arts and many duties at home are tied to religion

(Davies 2012, 267). Women spend much of their day creating and placing offerings for the home, village, and religious festivals. Beauty, duty, and therefore ability within society are all linked together. For the audience, Suprabha's beauty would serve as proof of her ability to assist Arjuna with his difficult task. She is beautiful and therefore she is capable—but her gender and the beauty associated with that also limits her ability to help.

In heaven, Suprabha is instrumental in defeating the ogre, but she does not ever fight him directly. After many rounds of battle, Arjuna remains unable to harm the terrible ogre. Arjuna then convinces Suprabha to seduce the ogre and in the process discover Niwatakwaca's vulnerability. Niwatakwaca is easily fooled when Suprabha promises him marriage—and he immediately gives up destroying the heavens for a night of pleasure. In the bedroom, Suprabha flatters Niwatakwaca's strength but begs to know where his vulnerability lies. She convinces him that telling her his weak spot would prove his love and loyalty and make for a happy marriage. Finally, Niwatakwaca reveals that his vulnerable spot is his tongue—an arrow shot there would kill him. Arjuna was listening in at the doorway and is able to burst in and fire the deadly shot. Arjuna celebrates his victory by marrying Suprabha (and several other heavenly nymphs, depending on the version).

The tongue, or voice, emerges as the central point of power and weakness in this part of the story. Suprabha is able to fool the ogre with her reasoning and rhetoric—she convinces him to reveal his weak spot, which is the tongue, the center of communication and voice. Scholar Sylvia Tiwon, writing about women authors in Java, argues that women are able to gain agency through "articulation":

> By articulation I mean the instance of giving voice, whether orally, in writing, or in print, to ideas and experiences, which, until they are voiced, especially in this age of competitive articulation, must remain private and thus, nonexistent as far as human society is concerned. Furthermore, when it assumes the existence of an audience, for articulation without an audience, though at times necessary, is, within the public function,

an absurdity, a negation of the human capacity and need to communicate. Articulation is also a function of the processes involved in the formation and transmission of cognitive and experiential schemata. Thus, it is not a static object, frozen within its own absoluteness. (1996, 48–49)

I have argued that the act of articulation in wayang kulit is more powerful than in other Balinese arts or literature because of the place it holds in society through its status as tradition. Articulation seems to propose the possibility of challenging oppression and creating a new status quo. I found, however, that challenging or changing tradition was extremely difficult to do in a wayang kulit performance.

Sexual innuendo and dialogues about women reflected how performance supports hegemony in Indonesia. After the first exchange between Arjuna and Suprabha, Twalen expresses his enthusiasm for going with Arjuna to heaven because of the many beautiful women he hopes to meet there. Merdah reminds him he already has a wife—but Twalen complains she is no longer beautiful and no longer of use to him. Pak Tunjung demonstrated a conversation between the two where the threat to the family could be paralleled with the threat the world faces if the heavens are destroyed:

> MERDAH: Father, this is a dangerous situation. If the monster is able to kill the place of the gods, then maybe he can kill us. I am so frightened.

> TWALEN: If the situation is like that, I want to go home. I want a long life! I can not forget your mother . . . maybe if we are gone for so long, when we come home you will have a younger brother with a face different from yours! If like that, I will know your mother has found a new "project" while we are away.

> MERDAH: Don't talk like that! You know that is wrong . . . and if you think and do like that, you are wrong too. You will make our family broken! OK, let's go— we need to follow Arjuna and save the heavens!

The scene Pak Tunjung modeled for me demonstrated how different levels of social order in Bali are connected within the performance. The possible destruction of the heavens, and thus the world, is reflected in Twalen's fear that his wife will be unfaithful. If Arjuna is not strong enough to defeat the monster, then Twalen is not virile enough to satisfy his wife. Indonesian history reflects this connection; Sukarno, Indonesia's first president, was seen as powerful because of his well-known sexual exploits (Anderson 1990, 32). For men, sexual power acts as an index of social power.

A later scene involving Arjuna, Twalen, and the condong reveals discourses surrounding sexual agency and gender. The scene begins with a dialogue between Arjuna and Suprabha in Kawi. The condong translates for Suprabha: "I have been waiting for many years to go away with a handsome man such as you. When a handsome man takes my hand in his, it is like I have gotten married and my dress becomes wet with passion." The dialogue, with its moist sexual imagery, seems incongruent with the chaste character of Suprabha, but in performance the condong character flits and flirts in front of Arjuna as she speaks these lines—there is slippage between the two women. The condong, with her dark skin and large bare breasts, is allowed to declare this kind of sexual desire, and in the next scene, she acts on it. I have seen Pak Tunjung perform this comic sequence numerous times. It begins with Arjuna and the condong appearing on the screen in a passionate embrace where Arjuna is standing behind the condong and his hands are rubbing her breasts. After a moment, Twalen appears and takes Arjuna's place behind the condong. The condong sighs with pleasure and turns around. The condong is surprised and angry to realize it was the fat, old Twalen trying to seduce her instead of the handsome prince. She chases him away, and in several versions she also heaves a large rock at him. The audience always laughed in delight at these scenes and at the condong's humiliation.

In practice and performance I struggled to "rewrite" these scenes in order to subvert the obvious sexism. I alternated between different versions where the condong would then get the best of

Twalen by hitting him with the rock, or I would allow the condong to fall in love with Twalen and chase him around. The rules for the penasar characters allow for the dalang to change the dialogue and action in many ways. Even so, I was not ultimately able to change the dynamics of gender and power inherent within the performance. Arjuna remained untouchable—I could comment on his actions in my performance, but at the end of the story he always emerged as the hero who married Suprabha as his reward.

Throughout this book I assert two primary and interdependent ideas: first, that change is a compatible and intrinsic quality of "tradition" that demonstrates tradition's relevancy for contemporary Balinese society. Women's involvement in wayang kulit can be seen as one example of change. Second, that those changes reveal tradition's special relationship to habitus, or the structuring structures within Balinese society. Traditions, such as wayang, constantly adjust in order to remain relevant and powerful in the present. I have argued for an understanding of tradition that accounts for its adaptability because as wayang kulit is learned and performed in each generation, the dalang adapt the stories and objects of wayang kulit to match the needs of its audience. I have described how this happens when Pak Tunjung selects a story or uses photocopies to borrow designs from other puppet carvers.

For the women characters in the wayang, sexual agency does not translate into power. Throughout Indonesia's history, women's sexuality contains a threat to the order of society. Like the characters on the screen, women who embrace sex are objects of ridicule, like the condong, or fear, like Rangda. Suprabha has power because she is both beautiful and chaste, but at the end of the story she marries Arjuna and disappears from the story. Like the woman dalang, who were brave to touch the puppets and learn wayang, Suprabha finds the courage to face the dangerous ogre. Tradition dictates that the better place for women is the home, and women dalang and Suprabha all end up returning to the domestic role that is their kodrat, or duty. Wayang kulit, even with women characters or women dalang, reinforces the social order as prescribed by tradition in Bali.

As women perform, they intervene into the "tradition" of way-ang kulit; over time will the "tradition" of wayang kulit evolve to better include women and their performances? Susilo, Bakan, and Kellar trace how the traditions of gamelan and arja are expanding and changing as women performers become commonplace. What does it suggest about the particular role of wayang kulit within Balinese society that this same transformation is not happening for women dalang? Why are women still in the shadows?

I began this book with a quote by Gayatri Chakravorty Spivak—arguing that women must be understood as a kind of subaltern who cannot emerge from the shadows. Someone else is always writing her history or defining the narrative of her lives (1999, 270, 308–9). The women who became dalang never fully controlled their opportunity or the conditions of performance. Each example reflects how tradition works in society and within social structures rather than demonstrating any real kind of equality within Bali-nese society.

Women dalang did not change Balinese hegemony but rather revealed the ways in which that hegemony functions. Spivak challenges others to speak for the subaltern, to resist complicity in the silencing of women's voices and expands the notion of speaking and acting in society (1999, 309–11). Spivak notes that, when dealing with the question of woman as subaltern, "the possibility of collectivity itself is persistently foreclosed through the manipulation of female agency" (1999, 270). Marvin Carlson's idea of ghosting—"entrapped by the memories of the public, so that each new appearance requires a renegotiation with those memories" (2003, 6)—haunts the ways in which a woman dalang disrupts the memories of tradition, of past performances and ritual. Her voice and body are denied access in the system—except where they become material indicators of extrinsic values such as equity and modernity. I remain hopeful about the future of women dalang, but in order for any significant number of women to continue within systems of dynamic practice, a change in the social systems surrounding the practice is necessary. More women in Bali are getting an education, waiting to marry, and leaving their families to work in offices and shops rather than toiling in rice fields and raising children (Davies 2012, 264–65). These changes are slow and are not yet reflected in the practice of wayang kulit. Only time will tell the future of the women in the shadows.

Notes

Chapter 1: Gender, Puppets, and Tradition

1. Pak (shortened from Bapak) is a title of respect for a man; it means father but is often used much like we would use Mister in English. Ibu, meaning mother, is the equivalent for women. It is stylistically common to retain the title of address when referring to men and women in scholarship about Bali, and I have emulated that here. I have dropped the title for close friends (who admonished me when I used the title) and do not use it when quoting scholarship by Balinese authors.

2. As far as I can tell, there is no actual law that allows the rider in pakian adat, or traditional clothes, to go without a helmet on a motorbike in Bali. The law requires all motorbike riders to wear a helmet. My friends and informants often told me, however, that no one wears a helmet with pakian adat, and I have never seen someone in traditional clothes with a helmet. Sometimes my friends would even change into pakian adat in order to avoid wearing a helmet.

3. Balinese religious and spiritual beliefs are based on the balance between negative and positive forces in the universe and the conviction that these forces are contained and controlled through human intervention such as ritual. These forces are called *ilmu pengiwa* and *ilmu penengen,* in (Balinese) or *ilmu putih* and *ilmu hitam* in (Indonesian), which mean "white magic" and "black magic" respectively. In my interaction with Balinese they almost exclusively used the term *black magic,* even when we were not conversing in English, probably out of the real fear of attracting these forces by using the Balinese or Indonesian term. Out of respect for that convention, I will continue to use the English term *black magic* in this book, even though I am aware that it contains unintended meaning in the West. In order to point out my use of this term in English I will put it in quotes to remind the reader that it is a specifically Balinese concept that I am invoking. For more on "black magic" in Bali, see Angela Hobart's *Healing Performances of Bali: Between Darkness and Light* or I Wayan Kardji's *Ilmu Hitam dari Bali.*

4. Hierarchy in Bali is performed not only through a language that changes depending on the speaker's relative social status to the listener but also indirectly, through the things that are said to given people in a given situation. Relative positions indicates status directly; whoever is in a physically higher position has higher status. Thus, when walking past people who are sitting, it is appropriate to bend over. My book comments on these direct and obvious shows of power, together with how language and action communicate and maintain hierarchy in less obvious ways.

5. In Java most of the audience watches wayang kulit from the same side of the screen as the dalang; often the screen will be up against a wall, making it impossible to watch the shadows.

6. I realize that even in the United States, the practice of sitting in a darkened auditorium to quietly watch a performance onstage is historically situated and attests to changing values within culture toward theatrical performance (see Levine 1988). In Bali, too, there is discussion regarding the "proper" behavior of an audience to appreciate a performance, especially in regard to the annual Bali Arts Festival, which often removed performances from their sacred context and moves them to a secular stage, where they are celebrated as art rather than functioning as ritual.

7. Throughout this book I strive to unpack the many ways "tradition" functions as a construct. Although I will not put the term in quotation marks each time, I urge the reader to refrain from taking this term for granted.

Chapter 2: Practices of Tradition

1. The initial and primary users of this concept are the media, specifically the *Bali Post* and *Bali TV*. Some feel the media even coined the term. For more on the complex discourses surrounding ajeg Bali, see Allen and Palermo 2005, 239–55.

2. My research focuses on Balinese wayang kulit, but shadow puppetry appears throughout Southeast Asia, and even in Indonesia there are several genres and types—each unique in terms of aesthetics, story, and purpose.

3. Wayang kulit can also be performed during the day; such a performance, called *wayang lemah,* is done for ritual purposes only and rarely is considered entertainment. Instead of a screen the dalang performs in front of a banana log affixed with a string strung across the playing area that defines and gives him a place to rest the puppets. One pair of gendèr will accompany this performance and the dalang requires only a single assistant. Even at a crowded temple ceremony there are very few people

watching wayang lemah; it serves primarily as an offering for the gods, and there are many ceremonies and occasions that require a wayang lemah performance.

4. Historically dalang have always been male; women dalang are a recent and rather rare exception. In order to reflect this I use the male pronoun when speaking about dalang in general and will use the female pronoun only when I am specifically referring to a female dalang.

5. Institut Seni Indonesia (ISI, Indonesian Institute for the Arts) offers S1 and S2 degrees (BA and MA) in puppetry, dance, theater, and music. Previously it was the Akademi Seni Tari Indonesia (ASTI, Indonesian Academy of the Arts) and then the Sekolah Tinggi Seni Indonesia (STSI, Indonesian University of the Arts). The Sekolah Menengah Karawitan Indonesia (SMKI, Indonesian High School for the Arts) previously was known as the Akademi Seni Karawitan Indonesia (KOKAR, Indonesian Conservatory for the Arts.)

6. My partner, and now wife, Tina, accompanied me on much of this research, and her presence is reflected in this book. We were not out as a lesbian couple to most of the Balinese we encountered—same-sex relationships are still strongly stigmatized in Indonesia, although close friendship with the same sex is common. Over time, most of my Balinese friends have come to understand the nature of our relationship, but because it was not something explicitly spoken about, I cannot make generalizations about my sexuality in relation to my research. Instead, I present Tina's presence as it is relevant and interesting—but I caution the reader about making any assumptions about homosexuality in relation to the arguments presented here.

7. In the summer of 2014, I was able to bring Pak Tunjung with me to perform at the UNIMA Asia-Pacific Puppet Festival, held in Nanchong, China. We won an award for group performance.

8. For more about historical and contemporary global circuits of wayang and their consequences, see Cohen 2007, 338–69.

9. Pak Tunjung began studying wayang with his grandfather when he was nine years old. After he turned twelve he also studied with I Nyoman Ganjreng. It is common for most dalang to learn from more than one teacher.

10. The Mahabharata together with the Ramayana provide the most common story material for a wayang kulit performance. These Hindu epics came down from India but are often modified slightly for a Balinese audience.

11. I first learned about wayang kulit when I was studying for my MFA in Asian performance and directing at the University of Hawai'i in a course on Southeast Asian performance taught by Kirstin Pauka in 2002.

12. Foley (2002) also writes about the relationship of teacher and student connecting past and present through the wayang performance. However, she invokes this relationship as a semiotic tool in order to understand the function of the performance and does not describe her learning process. I am focusing on the moment of transmission as a way to understand how wayang kulit operates as a productive force.

13. William Condee, who later studied wayang with Pak Tunjung as well, described a similar experience: "I don't recall him directly asking me for permission for touching me, but I do recall some sort of general 'ask.' I interpreted that as not a permission to touch me, but rather, 'I know you are an esteemed professor, but you have got this wrong. Please let me show you how to do this right.' In other words, the 'permission' was not to touch me but to correct me. I am sure you recall him saying, 'Very good (or OK), but a few corrections, please?'" (pers. comm., 2015).

14. For more information about how social interactions can be understood as an ever-changing performance, see Goffman 1959.

15. *Wayang parwa,* or wayang that tells stories from the Mahabharata, is the most popular type of wayang kulit in Bali. The structure I describe is from wayang parwa; other types of wayang might deviate from it, but wayang parwa is the norm to which other genres are compared.

16. For a detailed overview of the structure of a typical performance of wayang parwa, see Rubin and Sedana 2007, 30–32.

17. In the Hindu epic the Mahabharata, the Pandawas (sometimes spelled Pandavas) are the sons of Pandu and his wives, Kunti and Madri. The five brothers' names are Bima, Yudistira, Arjuna, Nakula, and Sahadewa. Their cousins are the Korawas, one hundred brothers all born to Gandari. Much of the action in the Mahabharata involves the rivalry between these two families.

18. In examining the discourse of Balinese aesthetics, I begin with the work of Stephen Davies, a philosopher, who identifies some of the key components of Balinese aesthetics. At the outset he acknowledges that a Balinese expert, Dr. Anak Agung Made Djelantik, has noted, "no writings about aesthetics specifically as a discipline exist in Bali." Even so, Davies identifies several key aesthetic concepts and ideals in Balinese culture and arts. In my own research I have observed that there is a developing Balinese discourse about aesthetics that foregrounds how much more important this conceptual framework has become within Balinese society. I will begin with Davies's categories and then draw from my own experience in order to examine how aesthetics and tradition are realized and understood within the objects of wayang kulit to demonstrate how these ideals regulate meaning and change. For more on aesthetics in Bali see Davies 2007, 27.

19. For a more detailed analysis of the objects used in performance, including the puppets, see chapter 3.

20. Even though Mrázek's analysis focuses on Javanese wayang kulit, it holds true for Balinese puppets as well and provides a useful way of thinking about the iconography of the puppets.

21. Original: *Tiga peran yang dimaksud adalah peran domestik (urusan rumah tangga), peran ekonomis/peran publik (mencari uang), dan peran social (tugas adat). Peran social merupakan peran yang tidak bias dibaikan karena berkaitan dengan kegiatan upacara. Peran social ini jauh lebih penting dibandingkan dengan peran-peran yang lainnya.*

22. Jenkins's analysis focuses on topeng, or masked drama, but his observations extend to the clowns of wayang kulit, as they are often performed side by side and are both required for an efficacious ritual.

Chapter 3: Objects of Tradition

1. From the "Ensiklopedia mini pewayangan Bali," an unpublished handbook of wayang history, mythology, and characters; my translation.

2. The translations into English that appear in many brochures, pamphlets, and programs distributed at Balinese museums, performances, and tourist offices have many errors in grammar and spelling. I have chosen to quote these directly as they appear, without correcting them, and I have also chosen not to use the word [*sic*] in order to point them out. Rather I wish to preserve the original text without distraction, but the reader should be aware that any errors seen in these quotes are intentional representations of the actual text.

3. Pak Wija did not invent wayang tantri; it was invented by I Wayan Persib, an arts student at ASTI, in 1980. Pak Wija, two years later, developed and made this genre popular (Sedana 2002, 28).

4. The students in the pendalang program study both Balinese and Javanese wayang kulit.

5. The idea of puppets as uncanny has recently received significant scholarly attention. For more, see Gross 2011; Posner, Orenstein, and Bell 2014.

6. For complex descriptions of the many personalities and forms the kanda empat can take throughout a person's life, see Eiseman 1989; Hooykaas 1973. My focus here is on how they work together with the dalang in performance, and I will limit my descriptions of these many forms and names in order to preserve clarity.

7. For a detailed analysis of the different parts of the puppet and their meanings, see Hobart 1987, 83–123.

8. The Balinese generally speak about "puppet gods," as if there is more than one puppet god. As I mentioned in my introductory note on language, Balinese and Indonesian are often unclear when it comes to establishing whether words are plural or singular. I have therefore chosen to retain the plural, because when it was talked about in English this is the form that was used. However, the precise relationship and identity between the puppet god(s) and the puppets as objects is one that requires more research next time I am in Bali.

Chapter 4: Ritual Traditions

1. I Nyoman Sedana, a dalang and scholar at ISI Denpasar, explained to me that holy water can be made using wayang peteng or wayang lemah (night and day wayang, respectively), but that stories from the Mahabharata were most commonly used. Sometimes other types of wayang might be used (pers. comm., October 2011).

2. Hooykaas (1973, 11–17) offers a descriptive overview of the different categories of priests in Bali and their relationship to one another within Balinese society.

3. Suratni is a dynamic and prolific performer. She performs regularly in *drama gong* (secular comic drama), arja (a kind of musical drama), and as a comic character in Calon Arang. In these performances she draws from her training both as a dalang and in topeng, or masked-drama performance. She most often plays an older condong, or comic servant character. Like other Balinese women, she also often dances for her village in temple ceremonies.

4. Bali is not the only part of Indonesia where women are performing as dalang. For more on dalang in Java and Bali, see Goodlander and Robertson 2016.

5. For an excellent overview of the dynamics of ritual obligation and community in Bali, see Warren 1995.

Chapter 5: Women Dalang

1. Luh De Suriyani, "Artists Must Fight Stagnancy, Established Ideas, Governor Says," *Bali Daily*, June 19, 2012.

2. Chapter XA, part 28A of the Indonesian constitution reads, "Setiap orang berhak untuk hidup serta berhak mempertahankan hidup dan kehidupannya" (Every person has the right to their life, together with the right to defend their life and livelihood). The rest of the chapter details more rights regarding family, education, religion, and culture. Parts 28H

and 281 are often cited as guaranteeing equal rights and responsibilities to all Indonesian citizens. For more on this, see Harijanti 2005, 79–81.

3. Like wayang kulit, gamelan was seen as primarily a man's activity, and only recently have women's and girl's groups become common, in spite of limitations and criticisms. For more on the history and context of the rise of women's gamelan, see Susilo 2003.

4. I am purposefully invoking the "past" in a general sense, because there are no continuous historic accounts or details of women and their specific roles in society. The Balinese I've spoken with understand there to be a shift in gender dynamics and social roles that began with independence and continues to expand. This is an area that requires more detailed historic research, but for my purposes a sense of a shift is just as meaningful as an actual quantifiable change in social roles and the arts.

5. Institut Seni Indonesia (ISI, Indonesian Institute for the Arts) offers S1 and S2 (BA and MA degrees) in puppetry, dance, theater, and music. Previously it was the Akademi Seni Tari Indonesia (ASTI, Indonesian Academy of the Arts) and then the Sekolah Tinggi Seni Indonesia (STSI, Indonesian University of the Arts). The Sekolah Menengah Karawitan Indonesia (SMKI, Indonesian High School for the Arts) previously was known as the Akademi Seni Karawitan Indonesia (KOKAR, Indonesian Conservatory for the Arts.)

6. Several of the women dalang I spoke with claimed to still be active as performers—but I made every effort to see women dalang perform, and such performances likely do not exist. I have been actively researching women dalang in Bali since 2008 and have watched only one woman perform. There was a women's competition at the Bali Arts Festival (PKB) in 2007, but I have only watched videos of performances. Sadly, women rarely if ever perform wayang kulit. My research, therefore, focuses on discourses of tradition within and around their performances and the tradition of wayang kulit rather than on detailed analysis of performances by women dalang.

7. Wayang kulit was not the only artistic genre being used as a platform to demonstrate women's equality through the arts by the state. Gamelan was and is used extensively in this way. Emiko Susilo states, "What is clear is that government support of gamelan wanita is related to the national policy towards women. Women were encouraged to play gamelan in the Bali Arts Festival to demonstrate that Balinese women are capable of playing gamelan, that they are able to do more than just work at home" (2003, 7).

8. For example, Ibu Nondri often performed for temple ceremonies, Ibu Trijata and Rasiani mention performing for rituals in their interview,

and I also watched Ibu Suratni perform wayang lemah (daytime wayang) at a village cremation ceremony in June 2009.

9. The oldest of these sons, I Wayan Mardika Bhuana, has become a very accomplished dalang and has even toured abroad.

10. For an excellent overview of this controversy and media coverage of Megawati's presidency, see Sen 2002.

11. It is not my intention to conflate Bali and Java into one homogeneous entity; there are many differences in society, religion, culture, and the arts. However, it has been noted that their systems for power are quite similar in basic structure and operation, and that is the focus of my comparison here.

12. In Indonesian there was a switch in spelling. The sound "ch" is now written by *c,* but it used to be noted with *tj;* therefore, there are several different spellings of Ibu Tjandri's name. In English-language publications it often appears as Chandri or Candri. However, she spelled it for me with the *Tj,* so that is the spelling I prefer to use.

13. Odin Teatret, in Denmark, is a highly regarded international company of theater artists led by Eugenio Barba. Through the practice of "theater anthropology," he and the other members of the company articulate a vocabulary of the body in performance through a consideration of traditional Western and Eastern theater forms.

14. Michael B. Bakan (1998) writes about a similar phenomenon among women musicians.

15. Natalie Kellar, in an article about arja and women performers, gives an excellent description of the condong: "The Condong is the Galuh's maidservant—a middle-aged commoner who is a mature, wise and loyal servant and the mistress's confidante. According to arts scholars in Bali, the Condong figure most clearly represents the traditional female character of Bali as nurturer, and upholder of morality. The Condong is regarded as half *halus* and half coarse or *kasar*—she displays quite a propensity for slapstick and often quite rough behaviour in her defence of the Galuh against the predations of unwelcome men" (2004, para. 35).

Chapter 6: Thoughts from the Shadows

1. For an excellent translation and background information on Arjuna Wiwaha, see Robson 2008. There are many variations and ways of telling these stories in wayang performance. I focus on the stories as given to me by my teachers, but they might vary from the source material or from how other dalang perform them.

Glossary

adat. Tradition or custom.

ajeg. A recent term to indicate something of traditional or religious importance in Bali.

alus. Refined.

arja. Dance-opera theater.

bale. A covered platform or pavilion used as a meeting place in the home or village (as in *bale banjar*).

balian. A lay priest or religious specialist.

banjar. The local community; cf. *bale banjar.*

bapak. Literally means "father"; used as a formal term of address for men, similar to "Mister" in English. Often shortened to "pak."

beleganjur. A type of marching percussion ensemble in Bali.

Bima. One of five Pandawa brothers in the Mahabharata. He is the biggest physically and has a quick temper.

Calon Arang. A ritual dance drama pitting the Barong against the witch Rangda. There is a popular tourist version.

cepala. A small wooden knocker that the *dalang* holds between his toes or in his hand in order to make percussive sounds during a *wayang kulit* performance.

condong. A female servant. There are also dances called condong.

dalang. A puppet master.

drama gong. A contemporary spoken theater performance with much comedy.

etika. "Ethics."

gambuh. Thought to be the oldest form of dance drama in Bali, combining music, singing, and dance.

gamelan. A percussion ensemble; uses different kinds of brass gongs, metallophones, drums, and sometimes flutes.

gamelan wanita. A woman's gamelan ensemble.

gender wayang. A small metallophone ensemble that often accompanies a *wayang kulit* performance.

guru. A teacher.

ibu. The polite term of address for a woman in Indonesia, similar to Ms. or Mrs. (lit., mother).

ISI. Institut Seni Indonesia, the performing Arts University in Denpasar; formally called ASTI (Akademi Seni Tinggi Indonesia).

kebaya. A lace or cotton blouse worn by women as part of *pakian adat.*

kaja. (Lit. mountain); refers to the sacred part of the island or the sacred direction.

kanda empat. The four brothers.

kasar. Unrefined.

Kawi. The Ancient Javanese court language used by alus (or refined) characters in a wayang performance.

kayonan. The large leaf-shaped puppet that represents the tree of life.

kelod. Refers to the sea, or the less sacred part of the island.

kodrat. "Inherent nature." The inherent qualities of a person.

Korawas. The 100 cousins of the Pandawas in the Mahabharata—often considered the "bad" characters.

malu. "Shy."

menyatu. "To become one."

mesakapan. A special ceremony where a *dalang* is "married" to his puppets.

ngayah. Something done as an offering to the gods or in service to the community.

niskala. The invisible realm. See *sekala.*

odalan. A temple celebration, often for the anniversary of a temple.

pak. The polite term of address for a man in Indonesia; similar to Mr. (lit., father).

pakian adat. Traditional clothing.

Pandawas. The five brothers in the Mahabharata, often considered the "heroes" of the story.

pedalangan. The study of the different arts to be a dalang, or puppet master.

penasar. The clown characters in *wayang kulit.* The four main penasar are Twalen, Merdah, Sangut, and Delem.

PKB. Pesta Kesenian Bali, the Bali Arts Festival. A large summer festival of performance and arts held in Bali every summer.

prembon. Dramatic dance genre created in 1940s, combining styles from many other Balinese genres.

pura. A Balinese Hindu temple.

raksasa. An ogre.

ringgit (Balinese). A puppet. See *wayang.*

sekala. The visible realm. See *niskala.*

SMKI: Sekolah Menengah Karawitan Indonesia (SMKI, Indonesian High School for the Arts) previously was known as the

Akademi Seni Karawitan Indonesia (KOKAR, Indonesian Conservatory for the Arts.)

taksu. Spiritual power.

topeng. A masked dance-drama performance.

tugas.upacara. The generic term for a special celebration or ceremony in Bali.

wanita. Woman or girls in Indonesia.

wayang. A general term that refers to many kinds of performances, but is also often used to refer specifically to puppets or puppet theater.

wayang golek. Three-dimensional rod puppet genre. Popular in the Sundanese region of Java.

wayang kulit. Wayang means "shadows" and kulit means "leather." The general term for shadow puppet performance in Indonesia.

wayang lemah. Daytime wayang.

wayang parwa. Wayang that tells stories from the Mahabharata.

wayang peteng. Nighttime wayang.

wayang tantri. Newer form of wayang that tells stories using animal puppets.

References

Allen, Pamela, and Carmencita Palermo. 2005. "*Ajeg Bali:* Multiple Meanings, Diverse Agendas." *Indonesia and the Malay World* 33, no. 97:239–55.

Anderson, Benedict R. O'G. 1990. *Language and Power: Exploring Political Cultures in Indonesia.* Ithaca: Cornell University Press.

Appadurai, Arjun. 1981. "The Past as a Scarce Resource." *Man,* n.s., 16, no. 2:201–19.

Bakan, Michael B. 1998. "From Oxymoron to Reality: Agendas of Gender and the Rise of Balinese Women's 'Gamelan Beleganjur' in Bali, Indonesia." *Asian Music* 29, no. 1:37–85.

Bakhtin, Mikhail. 1998. "Carnival and Carnivalesque." In *Cultural Theory and Popular Culture: A Reader,* edited by John Storey, 250–59. Essex, UK: Pearson Education.

Bali Cultural Office. 2013. "Museum Negeri Propinsi Bali." Pamphlet for museum visitors.

Bandem, I Made, and Fredrik Eugene deBoer. 1995. *Balinese Dance in Transition: Kaja and Kelod.* 2nd ed. Oxford: Oxford University Press.

Barth, Fredrik. 1993. *Balinese Worlds.* Chicago: University of Chicago Press.

Becker, A. L. 1989. Introduction to *Writing on the Tongue,* edited by Becker, 1–11. Ann Arbor: Michigan Papers on South and Southeast Asia.

Bell, Catherine. 1992. *Ritual Theory, Ritual Practice.* Oxford: Oxford University Press.

Bell, John. 1997. *Landscape and Desire: Bread and Puppet Pageants in the 1990s.* Glover, VT: Bread and Puppet Press.

Benamou, Marc. 2002. "Wayang Character Types, Musical Categories, and a Reconsideration of the Alus-Kasar Dichotomy." In *Puppet Theater in Contemporary Indonesia: New Approaches to Performance Events,* edited by Jan Mrázek. Ann Arbor: University of Michigan, Centers for South and Southeast Asian Studies, 271–83.

Berger, John. 1972. *The Look of Things: Essays.* New York: Viking Press.

Blackburn, Susan. 2004. *Women and the State in Modern Indonesia.* Cambridge: Cambridge University Press.

Bourdieu, Pierre. 1977. *Outline of a Theory of Practice*. Cambridge: Cambridge University Press.

———. 1984. *Distinction: A Social Critique of the Judgement of Taste*. Translated by Richard Nice. Cambridge, MA: Harvard University Press.

Butler, Judith. 1993. *Bodies That Matter: On the Discursive Limits of "Sex."* New York: Routledge.

Carlson, Marvin. 2003. *The Haunted Stage: The Theatre as Memory Machine*. Ann Arbor: University of Michigan Press.

Certeau, Michel de. 1984. *The Practice of Everyday Life*. Translated by Steven Rendall. Berkeley: University of California Press.

Clifford, James. 1988. *The Predicament of Culture: Twentieth-Century Ethnography, Literature, and Art*. Cambridge, MA: Harvard University Press.

Cohen, Matthew Isaac. 2007. "Contemporary Wayang in Global Contexts." *Asian Theatre Journal* 24, no. 2:338–69.

———. 2014. "Traditional and Post-traditional Wayang Kulit in Java Today." In Posner, Orenstein, and Bell, *Routledge Companion to Puppetry,* 178–91.

Cohen, Matthew Isaac, Alessandra Lopez y Royo, and Laura Noszlopy. 2007. "Indonesian Performing Arts across Borders." *Indonesia and the Malay World* 35, no. 101:1–7.

Conquergood, Dwight. 1985. "Performing as a Moral Act: Ethical Dimensions of the Ethnography of Performance." *Literature in Performance* 5, no. 2:1–13.

Davies, Stephen. 2007. "Balinese Aesthetics." *Journal of Aesthetics and Art Criticism* 65, no. 1:21–29.

———. 2012. "Beauty, Youth, and the Balinese *Legong* Dance." In *Beauty Unlimited,* edited by Peg Zeglin Brand, 259–79. Bloomington: Indiana University Press.

deBoer, Fredrik E. 1987. "Functions of the Comic Attendants (*Penasar*) in Balinese Shadowplay." In *Humor and Comedy in Puppetry: Celebration in Popular Culture,* edited by Dina Sherzer and Joel Sherzer, 79–105. Bowling Green, OH: Bowling Green State University Popular Press.

Diamond, Catherine. 2001. "*Wayang listrik: Dalang* Larry Reed's Shadow Bridge between Bali and San Francisco." *Theatre Research International* 26, no. 3:257–76.

———. 2008. "Fire in the Banana's Belly: Bali's Female Performers Essay the Masculine Arts." *Asian Theatre Journal* 25, no. 2:231–71.

———. 2012. *Communities of Imagination: Contemporary Southeast Asian Theatres*. Honolulu: University of Hawai'i Press.

Downing, Sonja Lynn. 2010. "Agency, Leadership, and Gender Negotiation in Balinese Girls' *Gamelans.*" *Ethnomusicology* 54, no. 1:54–80.

Durkheim, Émile. 1961. *The Elementary Forms of the Religious Life.* Translated by Joseph Ward Swain. New York: Collier.

Eiseman, Fred 1989. *Bali: Sekala and Niskala.* Vol. 1, *Essays on Religion, Ritual, and Art.* Singapore: Periplus Editions.

Emigh, John. 1979. "Playing with the Past: Visitation and Illusion in the Mask Theatre of Bali." *TDR* 23, no. 2:11–36.

———. 1996. *Masked Performance: The Play of Self and Other in Ritual and Theatre.* Philadelphia: University of Pennsylvania Press.

———. 2008. "Culture, Killings, and Criticism in the Years of Living Dangerously: Bali and Baliology." In *The Cambridge Companion to Performance Studies,* edited by Tracy C. Davis, 60–75. Cambridge: Cambridge University Press.

Emigh, John, and Jamar Hunt. 1992. "Gender Bending in Balinese Performance." In *Gender in Performance: The Presentation of Difference in the Performing Arts*, edited by Laurence Senelick, 195–222. Hanover: University of New Hampshire Press.

Errington, Shelly. 1990. "Recasting Sex, Gender, and Power: A Theoretical and Regional Overview." In *Power and Difference: Gender in Island Southeast Asia,* edited by Jane Monnig Atkinson and Errington, 1–58. Stanford: Stanford University Press.

Foley, Kathy. 1990. "My Bodies: The Performer in West Java." *TDR* 34, no. 2:62–80.

———. 2002. "First Things: Opening Passages in Southeast Asian Puppet Theater." In *Puppet Theater in Contemporary Indonesia: New Approaches to Performance Events,* edited by Jan Mrázek, 84–91. Ann Arbor: Michigan Papers on South and Southeast Asia.

Geertz, Clifford. 1975. *The Interpretation of Cultures.* London: Hutchinson.

Geertz, Hildred. 1994. *Images of Power: Balinese Paintings Made for Gregory Bateson and Margaret Mead.* Honolulu: University of Hawai'i Press.

George, David E. R. 1987. "Ritual Drama: Between Mysticism and Magic." *Asian Theatre Journal* 4, no. 2:127–65.

Glassie, Henry. 1995. "Tradition." *Journal of American Folklore* 108, no. 430:395–412.

Goffman, Erving. 1959. *The Presentation of Self in Everyday Life.* New York: Anchor.

Goodall, Jane. 2008. *Stage Presence.* New York: Routlege.

Goodlander, Jennifer. 2012. "Gender, Power, and Puppets: Two Early Women *Dalangs* in Bali." *Asian Theatre Journal* 29, no. 1:54–77.

Goodlander, Jennifer, and Ashley Robertson. 2016. "Case Study: Indonesian Dalang." In *Routledge Handbook of Asian Theatre,* edited by Siyuan Liu, 430–36. New York: Routledge.

Gralapp, Leland W. 1967. "Balinese Painting and the Wayang Tradition." *Artibus Asiae* 29, nos. 2–3:239–66.

Gross, Kenneth. 2011. *Puppet: An Essay on Uncanny Life.* Chicago: University of Chicago Press.

Guattari, Pierre-Félix. 1996. *The Guattari Reader.* Edited by Gary Genosko. Oxford: Blackwell.

Harijanti, Susi Dwi. 2005. "Indonesia." *Encyclopedia of Women and Islamic Cultures: Family, Law, and Politics,* edited by Suad Joseph. Vol. 2. Leiden: Koninklijke Brill NV.

Heimarck, Brita Renée. 2003. *Balinese Discourses on Music and Modernization: Village Voices and Urban Views.* New York: Routledge.

Herbst, Edward. 1997. *Voices in Bali: Energies and Perceptions in Vocal Music and Dance Theater.* Hanover, NH: Wesleyan University Press.

Hirschfeld-Medalia, Adeline. 1984. "The Voice in Wayang and Kabuki." *Asian Theatre Journal* 1, no. 2:217–22.

Hobart, Angela. 1985. *Balinese Shadow Play Figures: Their Social and Ritual Significance.* London: British Museum Occasional Paper no. 49.

———. 1987. *Dancing Shadows of Bali: Theatre and Myth.* New York: KPI.

———. 2003. *Healing Performances of Bali: Between Darkness and Light.* New York: Berghahn Books.

Hooykaas, Christiaan. 1973. *Religion in Bali.* Leiden: Brill.

Hough, Brett. 1999. "Education for the Performing Arts: Contesting and Mediating Identity in Contemporary Bali." In *Staying Local in the Global Village: Bali in the Twentieth Century,* edited by Raechelle Rubinstein and Linda H. Connor, 231–64. Honolulu: University of Hawai'i Press.

Hulsbosch, Marianne, Elizabeth Bedford, and Martha Chaiklin, eds. 2009. *Asian Material Culture.* Amsterdam: Amsterdam University Press.

James, John. 1973. "Sacred Geometry on the Island of Bali." *Journal of the Royal Asiatic Society of Great Britain and Ireland* 2:141–54.

Jenkins, Ron. 1994. *Subversive Laughter: The Liberating Power of Comedy.* New York: Free Press.

Kaelan, M. S. 2008. *Pendidikan Pancasila.* Yogyakarta: Paradigma.

Kapferer, Bruce, and Angela Hobart. 2005. "Introduction: The Aesthetics of Symbolic Construction and Experience." In *Aesthetics in Performance: Formations of Symbolic Construction and Experience.* edited by Kapferer and Hobart. New York: Berghahn.

Katz-Harris, Felicia. 2010. *Inside the Puppet Box: A Performance Collection of Wayang Kulit at the Museum of International Folk Art*. Sante Fe, NM: Museum of International Folk Art.

Kellar, Natalie. 2004. "Beyond New Order Gender Politics: Case Studies of Female Performers of the Classical Balinese Dance-Drama *Arja*." *Intersections: Gender, History and Culture in the Asian Context* 10. http://intersections.anu.edu.au/issue10/kellar.html. Accessed October 20, 2014.

Knowles, Ric. 2012. "Editorial Comment: Theatre and Material Culture." *Theatre Journal* 64, no. 3:1–3.

Lansing, J. Stephen. 1983. *The Three Worlds of Bali*. New York: Praeger.

———. 2006. *Perfect Order: Recognizing Complexity in Bali*. Princeton: Princeton University Press.

Lefebvre, Henri. 1992. *The Production of Space*. Translated by Donald Nicholson-Smith. Oxford: Blackwell.

Lendra, I. Wayan. 1995. "Bali and Grotowski: Some Parallels in the Training Process." In *Acting (Re)Considered: A Theoretical and Practical Guide*, edited by Phillip B. Zarrilli, 148–62.

Levine, Lawrence W. 1988. *Highbrow/Lowbrow: The Emergence of Cultural Hierarchy in America*. Cambridge, MA: Harvard University Press.

McDonald, Barry. 1997. "Tradition as a Personal Relationship." *Journal of American Folklore* 110, no. 435:47–67.

McIntosh, Jonathan. 2006. "How Dancing, Singing, and Playing Shape the Ethnographer: Research with Children in a Balinese Dance Studio." *Anthropology Matters* 8, no. 2:1–17.

Merleau-Ponty, Maurice. 1962. *Phenomenology of Perception*. Translated by Colin Smith. London: Routledge.

Mrázek, Jan. 1998. "Phenomenology of a Puppet Theatre: Contemplations on the Performance Technique of Contemporary Javanese Wayang Kulit." 2 vols. PhD diss., Cornell University.

Mulvey, Laura. 1975. "Visual Pleasure and Narrative Cinema." *Screen* 16, no. 3:6–18.

Noszlopy, Laura. 2005. "*Bazar*, Big Kites, and Other Boys' Things: Distinctions of Gender and Tradition in Balinese Youth Culture." *Australian Journal of Anthropology* 16, no. 2:179–97.

Palermo, Carmencita. 2007. "Towards the Embodiment of the Mask: Balinese Topeng in Contemporary Practice." PhD thesis, University of Tasmania.

———. 2009. "Anak mula keto 'It Was Always Thus': Women Making Progress, Encountering Limits in Characterising the Masks in

Balinese Masked Dance-Drama." *Intersections: Gender and Sexuality in Asia and the Pacific* 19. http://intersections.anu.edu.au/issue19/palermo.htm.

Parker, Lyn. 2005. "Resisting Resistance and Finding Agency: Women and Medicalized Birth in Bali." In *The Agency of Women in Asia,* edited by Lyn Parker. Singapore: Marshall Cavendish Academic.

Peacock, James. 1990. "Ethnographic Notes on Sacred and Profane Performance." In *By Means of Performance: Intercultural Studies of Theatre and Ritual,* edited by Richard Schechner and Willa Appel, 208–20. New York: Cambridge University Press.

Pedersen, Lene. 2002. "Ambiguous Bleeding: Purity and Sacrifice in Bali." *Ethnology* 41, no. 4:303–15.

Posner, Dassia N., Claudia Orenstein, and John Bell, eds. 2014. *The Routledge Companion to Puppetry and Material Performance.* London: Routledge.

Pringle, Robert. 2004. *A Short History of Bali: Indonesia's Hindu Realm.* Sydney: Allen and Unwin.

Robson, Stuart. 2008. *Arjunahwiwaha: The Marriage of Arjuna of Mpu Kanwa.* Leiden: KITLV.

Rubin, Leon, and I Nyoman Sedana. 2007. *Performance in Bali.* New York: Routledge.

Saussure, Ferdinand de. 2001. "Course in General Linguistics." In *The Norton Anthology of Theory and Criticism,* edited by Vincent B. Leitch, 96–976. New York: Norton.

Schechner, Richard. 1974. "From Ritual to Theatre and Back: The Structure/Process of the Efficacy/Entertainment Dyad." *Educational Theatre Journal* 26, no. 4:455–81.

———. 1993. *The Future of Ritual: Writings on Culture and Performance.* New York: Routledge.

Sedana, I Nyoman. 1993. "The Training, Education, and the Expanding Role of the Balinese *Dalang.*" MA thesis, Brown University.

———. 2002. "Kawi Dalang: Creativity in Wayang Theatre." PhD diss., University of Georgia.

Sen, Krishna. 2002. "The Mega Factor in Indonesian Politics: A New President, or a New Kind of Presidency?" In *Women in Indonesia: Gender, Equity, and Development,* edited by Kathryn Robinson and Sharron Bessell, 13–27. Singapore: Institute of Southeast Asian Studies.

Shadow Master. 2008. Directed by John Knoop and Larry Reed. DVD. San Francisco: Shadow Light Productions.

Snow, Stephen. 1986. "Intercultural Performance: The Balinese-American Model." *Asian Theatre Journal* 3, no. 2:204–32.

Spivak, Gayatri Chakravorty. 1999. *A Critique of Postcolonial Reason: Toward a History of the Vanishing Present*. Cambridge, MA: Harvard University Press.

Stephen, Michele. 2001. "Barong and Rangda in the Context of Balinese Religion." *Review of Indonesian and Malaysian Affairs* 35, no. 1:137–93.

Stephen, Michele. 2002. "Returning to the Original Form: A Central Dynamic in Balinese Ritual." *Bijdragen tot de taal-, land- en volkenkunde* 158, no. 1:61–94.

Sumandhi, I Nyoman. 1994. "The Bali Arts Festival: An Interview with I Nyoman Sumandhi." By Kathy Foley. *Asian Theatre Journal* 11, no. 2:275–89.

Suriyani, Luh De. 2012. "Artists Must Fight Stagnancy, Established Ideas, Governor Says." *Bali Daily*, June 19.

Suryani, Luh Ketut. 2004. "Balinese Women in a Changing Society." *Journal of the American Academy of Psychoanalysis and Dynamic Psychiatry* 32, no. 1:213–30.

Susilo, Emiko Saraswati. 2003. *Gamelan Wanita: A Study of Women's Gamelan in Bali*. Southeast Asia Paper no. 43. Manoa, HI: Center for Southeast Asian Studies.

Taylor, Diana. 2003. *The Archive and the Repertoire: Performing Cultural Memory in the Americas*. Durham: Duke University Press.

Tiwon, Sylvia. 1996. "Models and Maniacs: Articulating the Female in Indonesia." In *Fantasizing the Feminine in Indonesia,* edited by Laurie J. Sears. Durham: Duke University Press.

Tijata, Ni Ketut. 2009. Personal interview with author. 27 September.

Turner, Edith. 1992. *Experiencing Ritual: A New Interpretation of African Healing*. With William Blodgett, Singleton Kahona, and Fideli Benwa. Philadelphia: University of Pennsylvania Press.

Turner, Victor W. 1969. *The Ritual Process: Structure and Anti-structure*. Chicago: University of Chicago Press.

Van Gennep, Arnold. 1960. *The Rites of Passage*. Chicago: University of Chicago Press.

Vourloumis, Hypatia. 2010. "'My Dog Girl': Cok Sawitri's Agrammaticality, Affect and Balinese Feminist Performance." In *Contemporary Southeast Asian Performances: Transnational Perspectives*, edited by Matthew Isaac Cohen and Laura Noszlopy. Newcastle upon Tyne: Cambridge Publishing.

Warren, Carol. 1995. *Adat and Dinas: Balinese Communities in the Indonesian State*. Oxford: Oxford University Press.

———. 1998. "Mediating Modernity in Bali." *International Journal of Cultural Studies* 1, no. 1:83–108.

Weintraub, Andrew N. 2004. *Power Plays: Wayang Golek Puppet Theater of West Java*. Athens: Ohio University Press.

Wicaksana, I Dewa Ketut. 2000. "Eksistensi dalang wanita di Bali: Kendala dan prospeknya." *Mudra: Journal seni budaya* 9, no. 8:88–112.

Wiener, Margaret J. 1995. *Visible and Invisible Realms: Power, Magic, and Colonial Conquest in Bali*. Chicago: University of Chicago Press.

Wieringa, Saskia. 1998. "Sexual Metaphors in the Change from Soekarno's Old Order to Soeharto's New Order in Indonesia." *Review of Indonesian and Malaysian Affairs* 32, no. 2:143–78.

Williams, Raymond. 2005. *Culture and Materialism: Selected Essays*. New York: Verso.

Wiratini, Ni Made. 2009. *Problem peranan wanita dalam seni pertunjukan Bali di kota Denpasar*. Malang: Bayumedia Publishing.

Zurbuchen, Mary Sabina. 1987. *The Language of Balinese Shadow Theater*. Princeton: Princeton University Press.

Index

Mahabharata, 9, 25, 91, 100, 150, 179n, 180n
marriage, 54, 134–36, 145, 174–75; ceremony, to the puppets, 113–17
masolah, 38, 58
mawinten, 110, 111
Megawati Sukarno Putri, 155–56
menstruation, 109, 111, 152–53, 154
menyatu, 45, 46, 49
museum Bali, 66–69

Nardayana, I Wayan. *See* Cenk Blonk
Nartha, I Wayan, 91, 154
ngayah, 132–33
Nondri, Ni Wayan, 91, 149–56, 159, 166

odalan, 108, 128
offerings, 84, 94–95, 107, 108–9, 111, 112, 114, 116; for the puppets, 3, 5, 7–8, 20, 64, 98, 99–100, 105, 117, 129–30; women, 6, 54, 127, 138–39, 162, 170

pakian adat, 1–2, 107
Pancasila, 145
payment for performance, 8, 132, 153–54
penasar (clowns), 7, 33, 54, 55, 57–58, 85, 121, 169
percussion. *See* cepala
Pesta Kesenian Bali (PKB). *See* Bali Arts Festival
power, 12, 54, 56–57, 63, 69, 82, 83–84, 93–94, 149, 155, 171–73; beauty, 169–70; space, 120, 128–29
puppet box, 69, 70–75
puppets, 40–41, 69, 75; color, 80–81; conventions, 75–77, 78, 85–86; innovations, 79–80; making, 77–78, 81–82

Rama, 92–94
Ramayana, 9, 92–94, 179n
Rangda, 94–97, 173
Rasiani, Ni Wayan, 139, 140, 143, 166
reactions: to my performance, 61–62; to women dalang, 136–37, 154, 165

reasons for wayang performance, 2–3, 98
rwa bhineda, 17–18, 39–40, 117

sakti, 113, 122
Sangut. *See* Delem and Sangut
Sedana, I Nyoman, 22, 62–63, 104–5, 106, 128, 145–46, 153
Sekolah Menengah Kesenian Indonesia (SMKI), 22, 141, 144, 156
Setia Darma House of Puppets, 86, 91, 92, 94–97
shadow, 42, 83, 159, 174
Sidja, I Made, 92, 162, 164
Sinta, 92–94
Sita. *See* Sinta
social hierarchy, 4–5, 26–27, 45, 58–59, 71, 88, 104, 112, 121, 158, 178n
structure of performance, 33
Sumandhi, I Nyoman, 24, 121, 141–44, 146, 148
Suprabha, 168–73
Suratni, Ni Wayan, 122–23, 125–26, 127, 130–33, 161–66

taksu, 37–38, 49, 55, 73, 97–98, 99, 146, 151, 155
teaching, 21–22, 27, 30–33; and gender, 55–56, 138, 148; relationship between students and teachers, 46, 62–63, 131, 138, 145; at university, 22, 145–46
Tjandri, Ni Nyoman, 156–61, 166
topeng, 30, 58, 100, 125, 155; and foreigners, 23, 106; and women, 155, 156–57, 162
tradition, 8, 9, 11, 18, 73; changing, 8, 5–6, 7, 17–18, 25, 171, 173 wayang kulit as, 18–19, 26–27, 68–69, 173
Trijata, Ni Nyoman, 28, 139–40, 142, 143, 144, 145, 160, 166
tugas, 134, 145
Tumpak Wayang, 98
Twalen and Merdah, 45–46, 49–50, 53, 116, 135–36, 171–72; Twalen only, 45–46, 100, 173

ukil, 78
uncanny, 83

voice: in performance, 34, 40–41, 48–49; and power, 159, 170–71; women's voices, 142–43, 144–45, 158, 159–60, 164–65

wayang Calon Arang, 94–97
wayang lemah, 82, 124, 125–26, 127, 131–32, 178n

wayang Tantri, 25, 38, 80
Wija, I Wayan, 21, 24, 25, 80, 151, 154, 181n
women in Bali: other performance genres, 10–11; restrictions, 75, 85, 139; social roles, 54–55, 87–88, 135–36, 164

www.ingramcontent.com/pod-product-compliance
Lightning Source LLC
Chambersburg PA
CBHW021903020426
42334CB00013B/458